Crazy-Proofing High School Sports

John E. Tufte

ROWMAN & LITTLEFIELD EDUCATION
A division of
ROWMAN & LITTLEFIELD PUBLISHERS, INC.
Lanham • New York • Toronto • Plymouth, UK

Published by Rowman & Littlefield Education
A division of Rowman & Littlefield Publishers, Inc.
A wholly owned subsidary of The Rowman & Littlefield Publishing Group, Inc.
4501 Forbes Boulevard, Suite 200, Lanham, Maryland 20706
www.rowman.com

10 Thornbury Road, Plymouth PL6 7PP, United Kingdom

British Library Cataloguing in Publication Information Available

Library of Congress Cataloging-in-Publication Data

Tufte, John E. (John Elling), 1972-
Crazy-proofing high school sports / John Tufte.
p. cm.
Includes bibliographical references and index.
ISBN 978-1-61048-572-2 (cloth : alk. paper) -- ISBN 978-1-61048-573-9 (pbk. : alk. paper) -- ISBN
978-1-61048-574-6 (electronic)
1. School sports--United States. 2. School sports--Social aspects--United States. I. Title.
GV346.T84 2012
796.042--dc23

2011052496

The paper used in this publication meets the minimum requirements of American National
Standard for Information Sciences Permanence of Paper for Printed Library Materials,
ANSI/NISO Z39.48-1992.

Printed in the United States of America

Contents

Preface

Sports have played an integral part of my life from as early as I can remember to the present day. I remember playing "miracle catch" in my bedroom; this was a game created to use my bed as a soft landing for purposes of creating fantastic, unbelievable catches of footballs and baseballs. I know I was as young as six years-old, maybe even younger, when this invented game began.

Moments like this transitioned seamlessly to my first experiences with pseudo organized athletics—neighbor boys in the yard, meeting friends in the park, planning, organizing, playing like only the unsupervised can play. From there, the step to "real" teammates and "real" coaches was nearly too good to be true for me.

I remember my first team uniform, a green shirt that read "Badger Excavating" on the front and a little "4" on the back. This shirt was a badge of honor; I wore it with pride a little boy could not possibly comprehend. I loved sports, I loved what they represented, and I loved how good they made me feel about myself. I believe I was in the third grade.

It went like that for a few years. Sports were an easy friend for me. They were available, I was good at playing them, and I was rewarded emotionally for my efforts. The elementary years gave way to the junior high years, and sports remained a great positive in my life. I remember truly owning my athletic experiences when I was in seventh and eighth grade; no one drove me any harder at sports than I drove myself. No one would have even wanted to drive me any harder. And then I transitioned into high school sports…

I played three sports throughout high school, and I had little or nothing to complain about regarding my roles on the teams. My name was often in the paper for athletics, I was identified in school as an athlete, and I continued to work hard at sports in these years. However, it was during these high school years that much of the magic of playing sports diminished into something else, something I no longer controlled with ease. The passion of sports gave way to a different reality when I was in high school; gone were the days of "miracle catch."

My adulthood has included coaching high school sports for thirteen years. While coaching, I began to recognize the look of adolescents who have recently lost some of the joy of sport they held not too long ago. Unfortunately, these student athletes were (and still are) everywhere. I have come to learn that this negative transition is not only common, but very likely for high school athletes. With this, there appears to be a cause for the loss of joy in high school sports.

Adults, it can be concluded, are about the only thing capable of ruining youth sports for kids. There is an irony to the fact that high school athletes, at a time when they so badly need strong, mature, and consistent adult mentoring, are too often left in the lurch while coaches, parents, principals, superintendents, school board members, members of the media, and others make a mess out of what should be so very simple.

My own parents, whether it was intended or just because they were too busy themselves to dote on my every sport-related concern, remained wonderfully neutral alongside my passion for sports. I was encouraged to try my best, and I remember they were quite willing to lend an ear when I needed to share. However, I cannot recall ever having to credit them with any of my successes, justify for them any of my failures, or make them equals in my passion.

My successes in English, math, science, and music were emphasized just as much, if not more, than my sport accomplishments, despite the fact that I cared much more about sports than academics during that time. And when my Algebra grades were unworthy of the refrigerator magnets, I answered to it extensively. A missed lay-up? A ground ball through my legs? These were my issues to solve.

My mother and father allowed me to own my sports experiences, and I am quite grateful for the approach they used with me. Theirs was a philosophy of sports that many parents of today cannot—or will not—administer.

As stated above, I was both a basketball and a golf coach (as well as an English teacher) for thirteen years, so I am well aware that I may have views tainted by these coaching roles. During my time as a basketball coach, for example, I would often joke with my friends outside of the educational and extra curricular arenas that my social life had somehow never progressed beyond high school.

What that meant was simple: far too much of my time and energy was being spent with sixteen to eighteen year-old high school students in an attempt to win basketball games against other sixteen to eighteen year-old high school students who were also coached by grown men sacrificing their social lives.

Certainly not everything about high school sports from my adult perspective is and was a negative; in fact, some of my best moments as an educator came about because of an opportunity to coach student athletes. Perhaps for the remainder of my life, I will cherish the memories and many of the relationships with which I have been blessed because of high school sports.

And what am I to make of the waning passion and loss of ownership I experienced as a high school athlete? It was reality. In the end, I was an average high school athlete. "Miracle catches" do not happen on a regular basis (if ever) in high school sports for average athletes. Like the vast majority of everyone who participates in sports, I learned lessons about the real world and where I fit in it during high school.

I was not as good as I wanted to be in sports at that time. What separates me from many of today's student athletes, however, is that I was allowed to come to that conclusion harmoniously. I succeeded at times, I failed at times, and I was given these experiences to own as gifts from the wise adults in my life.

Today I make my living teaching, presenting, and writing. Although there is nothing whatsoever athletic about how I spend my working day, I am confident that my experiences in high school sports—both the good and the bad—have made me better at what I do. I truly hope today's high school athletes can say the same in twenty years.

Introduction

If one were to watch the entirety of almost any local news broadcast between the months of September and May, he or she would have a great chance of seeing video footage of and hearing expert analysis of athletes and teams associated with a high school. This has become such a norm within our culture that reading the sentence above most likely does very little to surprise.

Is this wrong? To answer this question is, perhaps, impossible. However, it can be furthered with more questions. Do adults who care about the high school football scores of late October show any interest in the reading or writing ability of the students within our communities?

Do those who know the student athletes personally understand as much about their class schedules as they do their hockey schedule? Does the public truly support what good can come from high school athletics, or are we simply interested in the final score as reported at 10:30 PM on the nightly news?

It only takes a few questions such as these to wonder if high school sports are too high a priority within our own lives or if we have mistakenly neglected that which is meant to be experienced positively in high school sports.

THE BENEFITS AND SIDE-EFFECTS OF HIGH SCHOOL SPORT PARTICIPATION

The benefits of high school sport participation are nearly without debate. There is an obvious and easily overlooked value to high school athletics that precedes the issues of relationships, communication, and roles of participants (the topics explored in this book). High school sports, first and foremost, are a form of much needed exercise for adolescents.

In a world filled with cell phones, iPods, video games, and high definition television, the need for physical activity is at a premium. There is an initial, fundamental truth about high school sports: aside from either a risk of injury or a rare exception to the rule, high school sports provide for its participants an undeniable physical benefit.

Along with benefiting physically, participants in high school sports also gain from what consistent exercise can do for one's mental health. Finding proof that high school sports can and will accomplish stress reduction, increase self-esteem, and possibly even work to relieve symptoms of depression may be difficult.

However, those who have spent a career in education, especially those who have been involved with adolescent high school students, could most likely add to the list of psychological benefits tied to sport participation. Many adolescents are better students and people because of sports. Exercise is good for people; it will not be debated within this book.

However true the benefits of exercise may be, the reality of high school sports goes well beyond the realm of exercising for health purposes. Important to this topic is the matter of what motivates high school students to participate in sports. Students in high school sports play sports, and the word "play" suggests reasons for participation other than improving one's cardiovascular fitness.

Kids play sports for more complicated reasons than simply demonstrating their physical abilities or competing at something—although they play for these reasons too. High school sports, for many adolescents, provide a social bond otherwise missing for many people this age.

For a great deal of high school athletes, the goal of winning games and competing at a high level is simply an understood reality of playing sports—and few high school athletes need to be reminded of the necessity to try one's best while competing. It cannot go without notice that high school athletes, when placed in a safe environment to tell the truth, clearly emphasize that the social connections gained by participating in sports matter more than wins or losses.

Further, these social connections are difficult to replicate away from the high school sports arena. In a world that provides every excuse to text instead of talk, watch instead of perform, and tune out instead of participate, high school sports bring young people together in ways that Facebook cannot.

All of this would be simple except for one major fact: it takes adults to run high school sports programs. And interestingly enough, adults do not benefit from high school sport participation the same way adolescents do. High school sport participation for adults demands absolutely no physical exercise. Nothing requires an adult to work well with others for the good of the whole during high school sport participation.

Adults have no "try outs" for team membership. Adults, further, can do or say nearly anything at any time to anyone regarding the school, the teachers, the coaches, the team, the players, the parents, or the media, and they are virtually guaranteed to have full access to their accustomed level of participation.

Meanwhile, the words and actions of adults are often the source of conflict for the student athlete. One student athlete, a seventeen year-old girl who started on the varsity team for three sports, described her parents' participation in her sports to me as, "a necessary evil." This is a problem.

THIS BOOK

Most scholars agree that high school sports are, by and large, a good thing for those who participate. This is not to be debated; however, taking an interest, or caring, in something like a sport can easily slide into something unhealthy, something often too ugly to recognize for those doing all the caring. Many people involved in high school sports—school administrators, coaches, parents, student athletes—struggle to find the balance required to care enough to benefit from sports while not allowing it to become a source of unnecessary, often damaging stress.

The purpose of this book is to deepen the understanding of high school sports and help those involved in the process better work together so that high school sports can be a wonderful supplement to a high school education instead of a source of angst and regret.

"Crazy-Proofing High School Sports" has two parts. The first four chapters complete *Part One: Where Schools Are—The problem is, we don't know what the problems are.* These chapters lay the groundwork necessary for improvement by making clear the issues hindering educators from what can and should be accomplished via high school sport participation.

Chapter one covers the issue of passion as it relates to everyone associated with high school sports. Specifically, the chapter details the differences between healthy, harmonious passion and hurtful, obsessive passion. For better or for worse, there appears to be no shortage of passion for those who participate in youth sports.

Chapter two details how student athletes, parents, school personnel, and other relevant participants view the purpose of high school sports. The varying perspectives are substantial. The third chapter describes relationship and communication quality and the vitality for each to be present in the high school sports experience.

Needless to say, there are massive voids of the necessary healthy relationships in today's schools when sports are involved. Chapter four covers success. What is success as it relates to the sports experience? The answer depends greatly upon who is asked.

After the first four chapters detail what the problems are with high school sports, the closing four chapters complete *Part Two: Where We Need To Go—Educators have everything needed to improve high school sports.* Chapter five reminds those in education the importance of knowing what needs to be done. If leaders in education react to the desires of the outspoken and struggle to instead lead, problems are unavoidable.

Chapter six urges educational leaders to have control, assign appropriate roles, and own their profession when it comes to the maintenance of high school sports. The seventh chapter brings back the issue of passion. It is the job of educators to teach perspective, whether it is to students, their parents, or themselves, when dealing with passions, and there is no better venue for this than the highly emotional realm of high school sport participation.

The eighth and final chapter of this book calls for the need to establish (or reestablish) the "school" in high school sports. Sports are an important aspect of so many students' lives. Educators absolutely must take steps to ensure that high school sports programs remain a healthy, vibrant, passionate supplement—no more, no less—to the high school education process.

Supplemental pages are included with suggestions for parents. Like educators, most parents want what is best for their child as it relates to high school sports. The best parental intentions, ironically, are often a great source of stress for their child.

These chapters are filled with a combination of what will best help the young people struggling through the difficulties of adolescence while facing the challenges of high school sport participation. This book draws upon research gleaned from other academics, extensive interview and observational research, my expertise as a high school teacher and coach, my years as a high school administrator, and a wisdom and common sense approach necessary for knowing what is best for kids.

Hopefully readers can enjoy these stories and find the words to be both practical and wise. However, when all is said and done, the purpose is only validated if the high school sports experience is made better for the young people participating.

Chapter One

Passion

PHYSICAL AND PSYCHOLOGICAL WELL-BEING

Educators and researchers alike have known for years that high school sports participation has tremendous benefits for student athletes. First and foremost, playing high school sports gives an adolescent the advantage of daily exercise. No one in education needs to ask if this is important; health problems such as obesity are apparent throughout high schools. At a time when video games and cell phones provide all the action some kids need to get through the day, sports are a blessed companion for anyone caring about the well-being of adolescents.

High school sports provide the backdrop necessary for young people to exercise diligently, eat well, resist damaging temptations, and adhere to a consistent daily schedule. Further, schools everywhere would have a physically healthier student body if all of its students were given such guidelines. Aside from either a risk of injury or a rare exception to the rule, high school sports provide for its participants an undeniable physical benefit.

The physical activity associated with playing sports also gives many high school student athletes an advantage against their non-participating classmates in the area of psychological health. Specifically, regular exercise in adolescents reduces stress, increases positive mood, builds self-esteem, and contributes to an improved functioning of the brain. Many experts believe that kids who play sports in high school are also less likely to struggle with depression or anxiety.

At the very least, high school sports have been shown to provide adolescents with an escape from negative experiences like divorce, financial struggles, and family illnesses or death. These conclusions are difficult to prove, yet those who have spent a career in education, especially those involved

1

with high school sports, could most likely add to the list of benefits, both physical and psychological, of sport participation. Exercise is good for kids, and this has absolutely nothing to do with why kids play sports.

SOCIAL BENEFITS OF SPORT PARTICIPATION

However true the benefits of exercise may be, the reality of high school sports goes well beyond the realm of exercising for health purposes. What motivates high school students to participate in sports? Students in high school play sports, and the word "play" suggests reasons for participation other than improving one's cardiovascular fitness.

Adolescents play sports for many reasons, but the most significant is that sports provide for these kids the social bonds they need to feel connected. My career in teaching and coaching validates this endlessly. High school sports give kids an opportunity to develop themselves physically, experience some excitement, and share these moments with teammates. Yes, high school athletes love to compete.

The goal of winning games and performing as best as one can is simply an understood reality of playing sports as a kid; no one needs to remind high school kids to try one's best while playing a varsity sport. However, I have found that from the mouths of high school athletes comes the information that social connections within sports matter more than winning, losing, or even accomplishing great personal successes.

The opportunities provided for student athletes in high school sports are difficult to reproduce elsewhere. In sports, these kids can throw themselves into a project and share the ups and downs with other kids who have chosen to do the same. These ups and downs, or life lessons, can reach the high school student athlete in ways that our classrooms struggle to accomplish.

Whether we in education care to embrace this reality or not, few classrooms can claim to play a significant role in improving a student's physical well-being, insisting they communicate effectively and with maturity, presenting them with opportunities to make good decisions, expecting teamwork, and helping them cope with mistakes all within a sixty-minute session.

Demands like those described, however, are common in sports. Interestingly enough, these are the very reasons high school kids love sports. Sports are difficult, a great deal is demanded of the students who play them, and the passion for these challenges can be a source of common-ground, a social connection to other students experiencing the same passions.

WITH POSITIVES COME NEGATIVES

The passion associated with high school sports would be simpler if the only emotions expressed came from the student athletes themselves. This is not the case, however, and two major details must be emphasized and discussed about the current status of high school sports and the perceived benefits of participation.

First, student athletes are not participating alone; they are joined by their parents, coaches, school officials, and the public. Second, when social and life skills are taught and learned through high school sports, there should not be an assumption that these skills are being modeled effectively for high school student athletes. These two details lead to a reality driving the need for this book: a great deal of the development from high school sports is unhealthy.

Early in the winter of 2010, there was an incredible article within an online newspaper based in Northern Minnesota. The article had a picture of five smiling high school girls standing in the gymnasium. The girls, all seniors, had recently been cut from the basketball team for various reasons.

The article was not specific with the details of the girls' removal from the team, but a word or two hinted that these players were becoming a distraction with behaviors unbecoming of high school student athletes. Further, the girls and some of their parents were quoted in the article. It was clear that these kids and their parents were displeased with the decisions of the coach, the school administrators, and the school district as a whole.

What the article failed to detail was something only those closely associated with high school sports would predict. The girls basketball team was a mess, and the five senior players removed from the roster, along with many of their parents, were at the center of nearly every conflict. Well before the five players were cut from the team, there were threatening phone calls made to the coach (by parents of these players), younger players were being bullied by these girls, team rules were being violated, and the list continues.

Those involved with high school sports can guess the source of this trouble because it is as common as any situation in team sports: the five senior girls cut from the basketball team were not playing as much as they wanted to play. Why? They were far less talented than the younger girls on the team.

Great educators hear of stories like the one involving the five girls, the basketball team, the parents, the coach, the administration, and the media, and they ask one very simple question: What did any of the kids involved in this situation learn because of this? Five high school girls were cut from a basketball team, and the next day their smiling faces are in the newspaper along with the story of how they were wronged.

Under what circumstances should any media outlet have latched on to this story? These girls, after both failing and being failed within a high school sports experience, found themselves getting attention for all of the wrong reasons—smiling for the camera because they would now be viewed as victims of decisions someone else made.

The list of wrong-doings within this story is daunting. How long had these girls been a negative distraction for the team? Why was their unacceptable behavior tolerated until well into their senior season? What could have been done before things got to this point? Clearly, the adults associated with coaching this team should be asking themselves these questions. With this, have any of these five girls been forced to reflect on their role in this mess?

Do these student athletes truly believe that the result of these events have nothing to do with the accumulation of their words and deeds? Clearly, someone in the lives of these children owed it to them to examine these questions. What about the parents? It is difficult to imagine that one day, out of absolutely nowhere, their daughters were cut from the basketball team and these parents were otherwise clueless about the steps leading toward this decision.

Nearly every parent of these girls met with the activities director privately after their daughters were cut from the team. One father sat in the high school office with tears rolling down his face explaining that now, because of the decisions of the coach and high school administration, his daughter will likely not receive a scholarship to play college basketball. It should be noted that before her removal from the team, this man's daughter lost her position to a girl two years younger—presumably because the other player was a better basketball player.

This father, only after his daughter's removal from the team, pleaded with the activities director and coach, promising he will make sure his daughter behaves appropriately as a member of the team. It is obviously unknown whether he actually believed his daughter's behavior was inappropriate or if he was simply trying any excuse he could use to get her back on the court. She was not allowed back on the team.

As a high school dean of students, I attempted to work with a senior boy and his parents after the boy was caught in a sticky situation. The boy, a senior hockey player, was a student in a video production class. The class was assigned a project to record, and the students were to turn their video tapes into the teacher's assignment bin before the end of the day.

Well after the school day ended and the teacher of this class had left for home, this boy asked a custodian to unlock the teacher's classroom so he could pick up the backpack he had mistakenly left behind.

The custodian noticed that the boy soon left the classroom without a backpack and that a previously locked cabinet in the room was now ajar. After days of investigating this event, it was discovered that the boy had mistakenly turned in the wrong tape for his class assignment. He was clearly concerned that his teacher get the proper tape, especially since the contents of the tape he reclaimed from her locked cabinet carried footage of himself heavily drinking alcohol with friends at a party.

What happened beyond this point is difficult to comprehend, even as I was involved first-hand. The boy eventually admitted to the scenario causing him to break into a locked cabinet in a classroom, not because he regretted his actions or wished to make amends, but rather because he was confident that what he had done was perfectly within his rights.

He explained that both tapes, after all, were his, and that he had simply wanted to retrieve one and replace it with another. He understood that the lock on his teacher's cabinet would need replacing and was more than willing to pay for this service himself. Further, he understood that he should probably have a detention or two for going about things this way. His parents completely agreed with his evaluation of the situation.

The parents of this boy were presented with the reality that their son lied to get into a classroom after hours, broke into a teacher's locked cabinet, and took back into his possession a video tape showing himself drinking alcohol (they watched the tape). They, like their son, concluded that the contents of the video tape were irrelevant to the school because if the boy had never been caught, the school administrators would never know about it—you cannot make this stuff up.

What makes people turn their backs on situations as serious as this? These parents literally looked the other way while the video of their son drinking beers at a party played in front of them. Why? Because their son is a hockey player, and getting caught in this light would mean a state high school league punishment with a minimum of two weeks of no games played. After exhausting all of his other arguments, the father of the boy said, "Well, clearly you can see this party happened last summer (the kids were tan and outside). You guys can't punish him now for something he did last summer. . ."

The boy was suspended from school for two days. He paid to have his teacher's cabinet lock replaced. The hockey season had not yet started. When it did, the boy served his state high school league suspension for drinking alcohol. Punishments like these are meaningless, however, without changed behavior. What did the boy learn from this experience? Who was to blame for his setbacks, the school administrators or himself?

There are intense, stressful conflicts associated with high school sports and those who participate in them. These damaging conflicts can involve school administrators, teachers, coaches, members of the media, community members, parents and other relatives, and, most importantly, the student athlete. But why does any of this matter? Why should educators, even those more removed from high school sports, care about what happened with the five high school girls basketball players or the boy who broke into his teacher's property to hide his drinking?

We should care because we are educators. Educators must embrace issues like these surrounding high school sports because we cannot allow young people to abuse or neglect their passions. Further, educators involved with high school sports are called to teach students, and in many cases the student athletes' parents, how to handle passion both when it is a source of joy and a source of disappointment.

At the forefront of both stories shared is sports. Further, in both instances, with an opportunity to use high school athletics as a positive backdrop for teaching student athletes to be better people, the situations deteriorated to the point where perhaps no one benefited.

TWO TYPES OF PASSION

High school sports elicit passion from its participants, including the adults who are not actually practicing or playing in the games. The passion extends well beyond the participants themselves, as well. We can find out which football teams are ranked in the state within five minutes of a news broadcast in early October; however, most of us would need a special visit to the principal's office for information about our local students' reading abilities, math test scores, and the percentage of graduates attending college. Right or wrong, people care deeply about the athletic prowess of the young people living within the communities we share.

As can easily be determined from the story about the five girls basketball players, the boy with the videotape issues, and the several stories to follow in this book, passion is a double-edged sword. Canadian psychology professor Robert Vallerand (2008) explains passion in a way that fits perfectly with the high school sports conflicts within our society. In short, there are two different types of passion: Harmonious Passion and Obsessive Passion.

Harmonious passion indicates that the person involved with the activity of choice—high school sports, for example—has freely chosen to participate and is in complete control of the activity and himself/herself while participating in the activity. When someone is participating harmoniously in a passion, the activity itself is significant but not an overwhelming presence within a person's identity. That is, the activity of choice is in harmony with the other essentials of the person's life (Vallerand, 2008, p. 2).

Another way people can look at harmonious passion is to ask a simple question about the activity in question: Am I, and are the people around me, better because of this passion? A wife and mother of two, for example, who runs three miles a day every morning to both keep herself in shape and have at least thirty minutes of alone-time is feeding an overwhelmingly harmonious and necessary passion.

Obsessive passion controls the person, plain and simple. Because of this, the person risks experiencing serious conflicts with self and others because of the passionate involvement within the activity (Valerand, p. 2). There is no test given to determine if one's passion is either harmonious or obsessive.

However, many of the proofs necessary for determining the health of a passion are held within the descriptors. A grown man who sneaks away to gamble money he has hidden from his spouse is obviously feeding an abusive and obsessive passion.

However, not all obsessive passions are so obvious to recognize. Are the moms and dads at the volleyball game in control of themselves or not? In what ways is the belligerent man at the football game affecting himself and those around him, those who may also have a passion for events like these?

Is it a healthy response for a high school junior to kick lockers and throw equipment after a loss, or does this boy need some guidance about how to handle himself when things do not work out like he wanted? Answers to questions like these can quickly lead to whether one has a harmonious or obsessive passion for high school sports.

WHO GETS TO ACT LIKE A KID?

The cup of passion for high school sports is overflowing. The problem with this is two-fold. To begin, and as it has been suggested within this chapter, not all passion is good. Second, many people associated with high school sports believe that the more they care about these sports, the better off these sports will be. This line of thinking has proven to become a mistake that is hurting the students playing high school sports.

What about the high school junior who kicked lockers and threw water bottles at the wall after a loss? Was this a healthy response? Of course not. Was it a natural response? Of course it was; it was as predictable as the sunrise. This player was an adolescent, and in the case of the boy referenced here, he was who struggled greatly to develop emotionally as quickly as he developed physically. This is adolescence in a nutshell, and although his behaviors cannot be tolerated, they absolutely must be understood.

Adolescent high school student athletes often find themselves in situations for which they are not prepared. Kids playing high school sports are still worried about the pimples on their chins and the fact that their third best friend chose to sit at a different table during lunch break.

High school student athletes, despite being treated like adults by many coaches, parents, and media outlets, are still struggling with the difference between how they see themselves versus how other people see them. It is cruelly ironic that while high school athletes are driving at break-neck speed to find an identity, their current stage in life makes complete harmony with many aspects of their life nearly impossible. High school kids are still kids, even if some of them look so strong and impressive while playing sports.

This is why and how a junior in high school can sound like a forty-five year-old man while being interviewed on television about the chances of his team succeeding in the upcoming tournament and twenty-four hours later resemble a three year-old throwing a tantrum in the locker room.

Educators should want student athletes to feel a passion for healthy sports participation. This is the purpose of high school sports. We want our kids to get excited and care about something, to learn what it feels like to prepare for whatever they believe is important, to feel what it takes to sacrifice for a goal, to experience the highs of success, and to deal with the lows of failure.

In short, we want high school student athletes to own the experience. And, of all the participants in high school sports, the high school student athlete is the one whom we expect to become obsessively passionate.

Adolescent high school athletes cannot help but sometimes care a bit too much about shooting baskets and not quite enough about doing homework. They will, without fail, react to a setback inappropriately now and then— schools do not furnish high school locker rooms with leather sofas and expensive lamps for a reason.

Adults, both parents and educators, are charged with teaching these adolescents how to handle their passions. Shooting hoops should never be a priority over homework. Kicking lockers should never be accepted as a sign of truly caring about the team.

Sports should never be an excuse to act like an idiot. Adolescents are going to act like adolescents; they always have and always will. This is not a problem as long as adults act like adults. Unfortunately, that has become an issue.

THE MEDIA

High school sports and the media have become fast friends. During the nine months of the public school calendar, nearly every nightly newscast will include scores, interviews, or insights about teams, athletes, or coaches from local communities. Clearly, there is enough passion for high school sports to justify the media attention it receives.

To the credit of most members of the media associated with high school sports, the coverage has maintained a level of decency and simplicity. That is, scores are shared, successes are detailed, and featured sections will often involve an endearing and inspirational story. Television, newspaper, and radio outlets will rarely dip into the suspended athletes, troubled coaches, and losing streaks of high school teams.

Despite the seemingly innocent presence of the media in high school sports, there is an underlying truth about making high school sports newsworthy that often plays a destructive role. If the passion of high school sports is already overflowing, having a coaches show on the radio every weekend for three months in the winter is not helping people keep things in perspective.

Do any of us really care enough about the local high school girls hockey team to listen to the coach, at 8:00 AM on a Saturday, mull over strategies for future opponents? We obviously do care this much, and that is troubling.

Yes, we should care about our kids and their activities. Yes, it is neat that the kids are given some attention now and then for their efforts and accomplishments. However, the media covering high school sports is, without apologies, a propaganda machine at its finest. Why? Because it is completely inappropriate for the media to be anything but a positive propaganda machine.

It was blatantly irresponsible and unprofessional for the on-line newspaper editor to write a story about the five basketball players cut from their team. With that story, and the picture of five smiling children on its front page, came a complete disregard for the fact that these were children; furthermore, many of these girls would live to regret their behaviors long after the editor of the piece moved on to a new topic.

Even the most seemingly innocent of our media-high school sports relationships are tainted with potential regret. During my years as a high school teacher and coach, one of the local radio stations ran a self-promoting advertisement for its broadcast of the boys hockey games.

The game announcer, a manager at the radio station, was an unabashed hockey fan—and his position, along with his passion for hockey, provided him an opportunity to run ads using highlights of his own play-by-play recordings. Every ad ended with a catchy little expression using a deep, raspy voice that only a radio station could use without blushing: "Otter Hockey ROCKS. . .On Z-103 FM!"

The problems with "Otter Hockey ROCKS. . ." on the local radio station five times an hour, every hour, are plentiful. To begin, it becomes a parody of itself. The high school hockey players were endlessly ridiculed by their peers (both athletes and non-athletes) for the cheesy radio slogan; even seventeen year-old students seemed to know that attempting to manufacture intensity for a game that is attended by less than fifty people on any given night is a bit silly. With this, the ad created animosity among parents and athletes of other sports.

Why doesn't Otter Basketball ROCK? How can the boys hockey team ROCK with a losing record, while the girls team has a winning record without ROCKING? There were even a few teachers who, at their best, would greet their classes on a test day with a sarcastic, "Otter Geometry ROCKS today!"

The kids who play hockey, and the community who embrace the sport, do not need to be convinced that hockey is cool. Style does not need to be sold over the airwaves to kids and their parents—they have enough already.

The media will continue to cover high school sports, and that is not necessarily a bad thing. Educators (coaches, teachers, and administrators) and parents, however, must be prepared to see media coverage for what it is and help high school athletes understand the tricks of the trade. The news will contain stories about winning teams and gifted athletes.

Coaches are always going to use their friendly, politically correct voices when they are interviewed, even if they sound nothing like this during practices or games. Sometimes the biggest jerk on the team will get the most attention. Most of the time people will only see or hear the tip of the iceberg, and it is almost impossible for the news to encompass all that truly matters about high school sports.

PARENTS

Twenty-five years ago, parents did not attend practices. Most parents back then could only attend a certain number of games, and most would find it difficult to travel on a Tuesday night for a basketball game halfway across the state. Parents were busier with other things twenty-five years ago; there was more than one child to support, even if he or she was not an athlete.

There was work to do both at the office and at home, and there were their own interests and obligations to maintain. These people were not bad parents, and their children in sports did not feel neglected. This is just the way things were in the not-too-distant past. Things have changed.

Organized sports were not offered to five-or six-year-old children when I was young. Sports were played at that age, but there was absolutely no need for adults to organize anything. The empty lot behind the house was a great football and baseball field, and the players were also the coaches and referees.

My seven year-old son was on a basketball team this past winter. During his practices, I intentionally removed myself from his line of sight by walking around a track above the gymnasium. What was witnessed, however, was often surprising.

Nearly every boy on the team had at least one parent present for the entire practice—after all, what is a seven year-old going to do, drive himself across town to the YMCA for basketball practice? The boys were a wonderful mess on the gym floor. They double dribbled, they traveled, they ran into each other at full speed, and they shot the ball from anywhere they could see the rim. It was what basketball should look like from first graders.

There were a few parents, specifically dads, who did not agree with this assessment. Grown men could be heard shouting at their children, "Dribble. . . Pass it. . . Shoot it!" and, as though the NBA finals were being decided, "Play defense!" There is no reason to believe that these dads did not mean well, and it did not appear to be ruining the experience for any of their sons. That said, it could be argued that the first cheeseburger one eats is not what makes him fat today. Things add up.

A closer look at parents who scream "play defense" at seven-year-old kids can be a good hint at what is to come in the future for both the child and the parent. There is nothing inherently awful about encouraging a child to do something better; however, it is a mistake for parents to take this significant level of ownership into something that is intended for the child.

My son asked me why I did not watch him practice. I explained to him that I look forward to watching him play in games, as long as he is comfortable with having me there. However, practice time must be his time, not mine. (I saw most of the practices anyway, but he doesn't need to know that right now.)

Where does this lead, and why is it such a big deal? If parents are deeply invested in the details of their child's sports success while the child is still in the early elementary years, the years to follow could be challenging for these parents, their children, and everyone else sharing the experience with them.

Stated differently, many parents believe they are supporting their sons and daughters by caring passionately for the sports their kids play. Granted, as the years pass, for one reason or another most parents will stop attending practices. Despite this, however, the passion many feel for their child's high school sports experience could only be rivaled by the passion felt by their child.

Most of the current crazy sport parents have forgotten what it was that gave them joy in sports as children. Further, the limited number of these parents who were actually considered good athletes have clearly forgotten how it was they became skilled at their respective sports.

Very few parents of current high school athletes had parents who endlessly taxied them around town, state, and nation for practices and games. When these parents were younger, they played in the driveway and the backyard, and they rode their bikes to the park to play a game with their friends.

Fewer of these parents, as children, were encouraged to attend summer sport camps to develop the skills necessary to "compete with the Jones'" and hopefully make it all the way to the state tournament in the coming years. Instead, they were told by their parents that money does not grow on trees and that an expensive football, basketball, or hockey camp is not going to make them any taller, faster, or stronger.

The irony behind many of the crazies is that their experiences with high school sports were purer and more fulfilling than the experiences they are so desperately trying to provide for their children. When it gets right down to it, playing in the driveway and in the yard accomplishes more than traveling 500 miles for a three-day tournament.

This is because experiences mean more to people, especially children, when they can be owned. Most of the benefits from sports happen when no one is watching. It is during these moments that student athletes dare to fail while trying something difficult. Furthermore, most of the fun associated with being a student athlete is dreaming about traveling to a tournament and playing well.

Where are these kids while they daydream? The driveway, the park, and the backyard. There is no room for a soft assessment of this line of thinking; it is not good for parents to care about high school sports as much as their kids care. The passion for sports belongs to children, yet it is too often owned by parents.

EDUCATORS

No one has a more difficult job to do in high school sports than the educators, whether it is the coaches, the teachers, or the administration. Student athletes are given a set of expectations to follow, and from that point their role is to play sports.

Parents and other community members, quite simply, are given the luxury of choosing for whom they most care, supporting this person or these people however they wish, watching what happens, and reacting to it as they see fit.

Great educators, however, are on the levee of passion, attempting to keep obsessive passion back so that the true benefits high school sports can provide for students are accessible. This passion levee will not break unless one of two situations happen: either the educators (coaches and administration) resemble the crazy sport parents and become obsessively passionate about high school sports themselves, or the the educators simply give up and allow the craziness.

Unlike having a passion for knitting, for example, having passion for high school sports is nearly impossible without being part of a relationship. Educators, specifically coaches and administrators, are the gatekeepers of relationships within high school sports, and it is evident that all of the relevant relationships for sports are a great deal associated with the passion of the participants. School district personnel are called to show empathy and responsiveness when someone is displeased with a situation relating to sports.

With this, they are encouraged to give the concerned public (especially moms and dads) a sense of empowerment so that school officials are not viewed as a rigid dictatorship. Last, educational leaders are expected to authentically handle the conflicts stemming from high school sports. These relationship-management expectations are often impossible for coaches and administrators.

Being crazy about high school sports is not reserved for "those" parents from "that" town. It is incredibly easy for a high school administrator or coach to find himself/herself doing or saying something otherwise out of character in the name of competitive passion. My research has provided opportunities to speak with several veteran coaches who lament the screaming, ranting, and raving of their younger coaching days.

These older, wiser coaches are afraid that theirs is a dying breed. As one coach offered, "With the way things are, who the hell is going to be willing to stick around coaching for thirty-five years and tolerate this crap?" His fear, he furthered, is that varsity head coaching positions will soon be littered with young men and women who have not benefited from the mentoring of more experienced, thoughtful coaches.

High school administrators have been heard debating the necessity of having an official school day while one of its sports teams is competing at a state tournament. Sentences like, "There is really no reason anyone is going to stay here anyway," may not sound awful at first, but a closer examination can put some perspective into how much value educators may be giving sports. Older, wiser, Hall of Fame caliber coaches understand the vitality of a full day of academics, and most of them value a typical Thursday evening practice as much as any game night.

When I worked as a high school dean of students, there were two other administrators in the main office, the principal and the activities director. During our three years together, I worked with student discipline and attendance issues, the activities director concentrated on extra-curricular activities, and the principal was the academic leader of the school and assisted the activities director and me during hectic moments.

In a school with over 700 adolescents, the likelihood of attendance concerns and behavioral issues was strong, and there were frequent, necessary discussions with parents. I met with parents nearly every day and spent hours speaking with others on the phone. However, the vast majority of my discussions with parents were initiated by me.

That was not the case for the activities director. He too met with parents nearly every day, and, like me, he worked to mend some relationship fences so that the system could run smoothly. In his case, however, the problems were brought to him. The parents of high school athletes did not wait for trouble to blow over; they sought to find a solution (and they usually had one in mind) quickly. The number of grown men and women who left their jobs in the middle of the day to speak to our activities director about a sports conflict is staggering.

And what about the principal? In three years, the principal met with one parent about academics at the high school. One. This is not to say the principal sat in his office and cruised the internet all day. In fact, he was an amazing asset to the school by working with his colleagues, especially the activities director and me, to build a healthy school philosophy and keep the "crazies" at bay.

His academic vision for both teachers and students was rigorous and insightful. However, it can not go without emphasis that one parent in three years entered a school serving over 700 students for the purpose of discussing academics. This is the world in which educators live.

WHAT EVERYONE CARES ABOUT

Many in education have been lulled into agreeing that, because people "care" a great deal about something associated with schools, it must be acceptable and worthwhile and educationally sound. This is flawed thinking. It is unacceptable for leaders in education to dote on the every want and need of students, parents, and even coaches as it relates to their concerns for sports. Not every meeting Mr. and Mrs. Jones demand to have with the coach and the activities director requires the school's obligation.

Not every accomplishment involving athletics requires a pep rally. Not every teacher should be fine with struggling students consistently leaving school early in the spring to compete in a sporting event. There are countless examples making the point that inappropriate, obsessive passion for anything related to education is worse than no passion at all. One needs to look no further than a great classroom teacher to illustrate this point.

Mr. Hurley has been science teacher at East Grand Forks Senior High School (northern Minnesota) for nearly thirty years, and he is nothing short of incredible. He is intelligent, confident, friendly, loud, insightful, and a bit odd all while helping adolescent students understand the delicate nature of things like the human reproductive system—and he removes all of the need to squirm in the desk with the topic's discomfort because he beats every kid to the adolescent punch-line before the kid even thinks about saying it. "Yes, these images are testes." "Yes, these are ovaries." "Yes, in this class we will say the word 'erection' without giggling like a bunch of fifth graders." This man was made to teach high school students.

I was a sophomore in high school when I sat in Mr. Hurley's science class. It was fifth period. I sat next to Becky, whom I adored for every reason sophomore boys like girls. There I sat next to Becky, learning about the male and female reproductive systems while both wanting to die and wanting to learn what Mr. Hurley was going to share with us next.

I swear he knew; he had to have known because of the look he gave me now and then as though to say, "Hang in there, son, we're almost done. . ." Soon the human reproductive unit was behind us, yet the magic of Mr. Hurley's teaching remained. Coming to fifth period was wonderful, and sitting next to Becky was only a small part of it.

The irony about referencing Mr. Hurley's science class at this point in my life is that I hardly ever talked about it with anyone while I was his student. My passions as a sophomore in high school were outside of academia. I sang in the school choir, performing on stage with various groups, and I played basketball. These activities, especially basketball, were the sources of my conversations with friends and family.

These activities were what my parents paid to see. Basketball was what I endlessly practiced in my driveway while daydreaming about making the winning shot. Success in basketball could make me glow, and failure would often bring me to tears. Science class is what I enjoyed for fifty minutes a day, five days a week.

Science class is not a source of passion for a sophomore in high school; it simply does not work that way for most kids. Some students may go home at night and talk to their parents about that wild and whacky Mr. Hurley, but they will come nowhere near adequately describing the totality of what he accomplishes as a teacher.

Because of this reality, most of the public does not care about what Mr. Hurley does in his classroom. No parent is calling the current principal at East Grand Forks Senior High School about Mr. Hurley's teaching. Why? Because he is doing a good job. The combination of academics and the absence of conflict will keep the phones from ringing at any school.

So why is it that over twenty years after graduating from high school, I am now drawn to remember Mr. Hurley's class as fondly as I recall any moments on the basketball court? Quite simply, I am not a kid anymore, and my white-hot passions as a sophomore in high school have been put in perspective for me as a grown man.

Educators are wise to remember that life does not end at high school graduation for student athletes. Everyone obviously knows this, but it is not always reflected in the decision making at schools. People get passionate about sports, and school officials and coaches are often blind to the consequences of allowing these people to "care" themselves and their children into a stupor.

Clearly, one of the major sources of conflict in high school sports today is that people are given the benefit of the doubt when it comes to caring deeply about their sports experiences. Unfortunately, these passions often come at the cost of what makes sense for kids both now and for the future. Educators must remember that Mr. Hurley is still making an incredible impact on students who may not talk about him for years.

YOUR PASSION IS KILLING MY PASSION

What is the smartest move a mom and dad can make when they dislike the boy their high school daughter wants to date? The move is simple; all they need to do is rant and rave to their daughter about how much they like the boy.

Jokes aside, there is a message in this one that can ring true in the world of high school sports and its participants. Just as a high school girl does not want or need her parents to love her boyfriend as much as she does, kids do not need help being passionate about anything they choose to do; they need help keeping it under control.

There is something terribly sad about a seventeen-year-old kid who, despite having enough talent to play a significant role on a high school sports team, will not join the team because he cannot imagine having it be worthwhile. How does this happen? Aside from lingering academic concerns, dramatic social issues with teammates, or a battle with depression, there is really only one way this happens: adults and obsessive passion. Countless talented high school student athletes have lost their spark for sports because the adults in their lives have created a forest-fire.

The vast majority of everyone associated with high school sports are good, well-intended people. Nobody coaches to see their student athletes miserable. No parents want to ruin a healthy experience for their child. No administrators want to lead in a manner that detracts from what is best for the student. Passion, however, can turn the best of intentions into a source of conflict. The remaining contents of this book must all be considered with passion as a backdrop.

Chapter Two

Great Teachers

Legendary coach John Wooden referenced "intentness" as a necessary building block for success. In Wooden's eyes, having intentness meant resisting the relentless temptations confronting us and, consequently, avoiding the distractions that keep us from our goals. Having tremendous intentness, or an immense fight, can serve people well and lead them to great accomplishments. Where did it lead John Wooden?

Ten national championships at the highest level of college basketball requires absolutely no elaboration. It is ironic, however, that this impressive supply of grit, nose to the grindstone, never back down intentness can cripple a group of people trying to work together easier than it can lead them to greatness. This can happen for one reason: the people cannot agree on how to focus their collected intentness.

If people involved in something evoking great passion cannot participate with a unified purpose, there will be conflict. Unfortunately, this conflict can often overshadow any benefits associated with the activity. In coach Wooden's prime, he dedicated practice time to instructing his players with the proper method of putting on their socks.

This reportedly drove many of his players to the edge of their sanity. When one of his elite players, Bill Walton, informed Wooden that the team expectation for a short haircut was ridiculous and not a standard worth following, Wooden explained his regret that Walton would be leaving the team and that he wished him nothing but the best. Bill Walton cut his hair.

How did John Wooden, perhaps the most revered coach of all time and in any sport, win ten national championships with an intentness that made many of his best players bite their tongue? There was a purpose to John Wooden's methods, and if the young men on his team wanted to play for UCLA they were going to have this purpose as well.

Wooden's players were going to focus on the process of doing all the little things well, from tying their shoes to completing a drill without dropping the ball. From there, he thought, the bigger things, like winning games, would be nothing more than symptoms of doing the little things correctly.

Along with this purpose, however, came a reality absent from the usual John Wooden lore. If Bill Walton's mom or dad called UCLA to complain about Coach Wooden's haircut policy, no one answered the phone. The coach was the teacher, the players were the students, and these were the only people required to accomplish the goals.

Stories like those told about UCLA's greatness behind the leadership of John Wooden are great reminders that establishing and maintaining a common purpose within a group is easier when the group shares a purpose. The accomplishments, furthermore, can be impressive when the group's leader (or leaders) is/are great.

This reality is apparent outside of sports as well. Great teachers accomplish feats in the classroom that other teachers cannot. There may be several reasons for this, but paramount to any teacher's success is the ability he or she has to have everybody on the same page at the same time. In our best classrooms, the focus is clear. There is a unified purpose between and among the teacher and students; therefore, a target is given and all are headed in that direction.

This is not to suggest that the students in every great teacher's classroom have a complete understanding of the purpose for every lesson taught, nor are these students in a position to advise the teacher on subject material or how it should be taught. Rather, great teachers have earned a necessary trust from their students. Students in these classrooms know that what they are learning or doing will come together and make sense to them when the time is right. They know this because a successful outcome has been consistently reinforced by the great teacher leading the class.

Mr. Jurgens is a high school social studies and psychology teacher in Fergus Falls, Minnesota. His knowledge and comprehension of history, geography, current events, and psychology is likely no more impressive than any other teacher with comparable preparation and years of experience. He knows his content, certainly, but that has little to do with why he is great in the classroom.

Mr. Jurgens consistently accomplishes more with his students than many teachers even dare to try. There is a "feel" to his classroom that lends itself to student improvement, and a comfort level is provided for students to be the best versions of themselves for the hour they are in his desks.

Adolescents who are known to crave inappropriate attention sit with their comments to themselves, respectful of the needs of others in Mr. Jurgens' class. Terribly shy and insecure kids are made to feel like they matter in his class. These students often seek him before and after the period to discuss both the subject material and various other issues they may be facing. Student athletes know they will not be treated as royalty, despite the fact that Mr. Jurgens has been very active as a coach in several high school sports.

The most gifted and popular students are charged with the responsibility of deserving their talents in Mr. Jurgens' presence, and because of this demand he places on them, they become better students and people. There are some really fun topics to study, and Mr. Jurgens wants everyone to benefit from these without the unnecessary distractions so many other teachers (and some administrators) tolerate.

How does he accomplish these things? It is purposeful. Great teachers know what they want to accomplish, and they work with their students to get it done. Students follow his lead because his expectations make sense, his message is consistent and clear, and there is a feeling of success coming from Mr. Jurgens' classroom that lends itself to even more success. Kids trust Mr. Jurgens.

OTHER TEACHERS

What about some of the other classrooms in schools, where despite the presence of an immensely knowledgeable teacher within his or her subject area, there appears to be a roadblock to success? In many of these classrooms, the students do not have a purpose for doing what they should be doing. Students in these classrooms are often predictably unruly, they struggle to flourish with assignments and tests, and at times they may refuse to participate in any fashion—unless, of course, they are allowed to participate on their terms only.

This reality is likely because the teacher either has failed to convey a vital sense of purpose to the class, or worse yet, the teacher himself does not know the purpose. Either way, without an agreed upon sense of purpose, no target is given, students head in vastly different directions, and failure follows.

Many teachers do not realize that they have been given nearly as much opportunity for establishing a purpose as John Wooden had as a basketball coach. Wooden, as amazing as his skills were as a coach, benefited from the reality that he was clearly in control of his team.

Parents of players had absolutely no leverage or decision making of any sort for Wooden's teams. Once a young man became a UCLA Bruin, he was either destined to join John Wooden down one path or take another path back home or to another university.

Mr. Jurgen's psychology class, at its core, is no different. It is not because parents are turned away at the door and told their voices are unwanted and unneeded. Rather, it is because psychology class (along with all the other courses offered) is not where parents are investing any of their passions.

Every year brings stories of high school coaches removed from their positions by the school board, a group of local folks who have been inundated by players' parents to take action. Few of these removed coaches lose their teaching positions, however.

It is strange that a man or woman can be deemed unfit for coaching while simultaneously maintaining a level of excellence as a classroom teacher. The truth is actually much more disturbing. The parents and school boards who have coaches removed from their positions have no idea how well these people teach; furthermore, they most likely have very little insights into their coaching abilities.

Coaches are fired because children become disappointed while playing a sport, and sports should not disappoint the children of some people. Teachers, whether they are good, great, or awful, do not inspire enough passion from parents within a community to be removed or replaced. Although this is an unfortunate reality in our schools, great teachers like Mr. Jurgens have utilized the freedom of the classroom to accomplish amazing feats while no one has been watching.

Are any students ever disappointed in Mr. Jurgens' classes? Absolutely. When adolescents are inappropriate in his presence, they are corrected and their behavior changes. This is purposeful for Mr. Jurgens. This is what good teachers of adolescents do. If his classes were high school sports, however, he would likely be unemployed.

HIGH SCHOOL SPORTS

While it is possible for classroom teachers, outside of extreme public focus, to educate students with a meaningful purpose, and consequently have students identify with these ideologies, it is becoming nearly impossible for educators to accomplish anything near this with high school sports.

Participation in high school sports with student athletes, coaches, administrators, teachers, and parents is at an all-time high, and in many ways this is great. However, one the major problems with high school sports today is the incredible number of cooks in the kitchen—and they are all trying to make their own supper.

Educators, student athletes, and parents do not share a philosophy of purpose for high school sports; therefore, they participate with vastly differing expectations. There are a number of divisions between and among participants. Some parents view the purpose of sports differently than other parents, high school kids do not always share a purpose with their peers, and educators even struggle to agree with a unified vision for the purpose of sport.

These inconsistencies are profound, yet they are merely the subtle differences some in a group have with others within the same group. It is easy to imagine how conflicts can emerge, therefore, when parents disagree with educators, educators try to support some parents while battling others, and student athletes are stuck in the middle trying to make sense of high school sports while they are strapped with the burden of adolescence.

STUDENT ATHLETES AND PURPOSE

"Probably the friendships. I basically play hockey for the friendships." This quote comes from Ned, who at the time was a talented starting goalie for his high school hockey team. Why do you play sports? What is the purpose? Student athletes cannot answer questions like these fast enough, and their responses are surprising.

Paul, a high school junior, offered the following when asked why he plays sports, "It's another good way to get to know people better and how to work with other people, not just in a school environment. . .it gives you good skills with that. . .and I like to compete." The acknowledgment of enjoying competition came from Paul as an afterthought, somewhere behind the social benefits of sport participation.

Christine, a senior and starter on her basketball team, added to this view of purpose: "It's all about a learning experience, taking responsibility for your actions. It's about relationships with different people, not only on the court, but off the court. . ." Again, absent from the words of this student athlete was any focus on personal accolades, or winning and losing, or even the sport itself.

Ned, quoted above regarding his purpose for playing hockey, also admitted that he played sports "probably for the physical activity—so I have something to do so that I don't get myself into trouble, the crap that kids get into..." When urged to explain what some kids "get into," Ned explained that many high school students do drugs and alcohol, and "there are more temptations if you don't do sports."

There is a significance in the responses of these student athletes. Why do they play sports? Of what purpose does sport have for them as high school student athletes? Nearly every student athlete interviewed answered questions like these by focusing on more than the sport itself. The student athletes view high school sports as a social avenue which they hope will be a positive force within their lives. The idea of being part of a team and having common goals with their peers, furthermore, feels good for these kids.

Are the student athletes saying these words because that is what they think they should be saying? Perhaps. Not many seventeen year-old children are comfortable admitting that their purpose for playing football is to endlessly destroy and embarrass an opponent. However, as it is possible for adolescent high school student athletes to be tamed into political correctness as he or she speaks to an adult, it is also necessary to validate their words by studying their actions.

Most of the adults involved with high school sports only see the student athletes perform (and behave) during games. In fact, only the high school coaches and the athletes themselves have consistent access to sport participation outside of the official games against opponents from another school.

Why does this matter as it relates to how high school kids see the purpose of sport? Because competition breeds stress, and stress seldom brings out the best in anyone during high school sports—especially if one's team is on the losing end of the competition.

It is natural to question the authenticity of "I basically play hockey for the friendships," until we are given the opportunity to observe student athletes in the bus after a game, in the locker room before practice, and during a practice itself. The stress of trying to win on game nights often places student athletes at the mercy of the situation.

If they win and everyone is happy, they too will likely be happy (this is not a guarantee, however). If they lose and many are distraught, they too will reflect this emotion. Practices and locker rooms and bus rides, to name a few, have different stories to tell. This is where student athletes often show their smiles, joke with their friends, and find the release they need at the end of the day.

There is no better time to determine the purpose of high school sports for kids than the day after their season ends. In a basketball season, for example, most teams (and therefore most players) end every season with a loss. There are sorrowful hugs on the court, there are tears in the locker room, and sometimes the quiet lasts as long as the bus ride home. However, the players bounce back the next day better than most of the adults associated with the team.

Some start preparing for track season. A few play tennis. Some others revel in the idea of going straight home and doing nothing after school. Sure, they are sad to have something end that was so dear to them, but none of these players are lost without basketball. As long as the social connections are maintained, the purpose of high school sports can be accomplished for student athletes – even when they are not participating in the sports.

It is worth noting that of the three groups studied and interviewed for this book, educators, student athletes, and parents, the student athletes are by far and away the most consistent with their words and actions. The joys of competition are the assumption for student athletes; they participate for relationships.

PARENTS AND PURPOSE

"You don't remember the win and loss record, you remember the relationships you've built with your coach and your teammates." These words about what kids should gain from high school sports come from Larry, a parent interviewed for this book. Larry appeared to be an exception to the rule as it pertains to sport parents.

Clearly, Larry is different from the typical parent of a high school athlete. His age (he is older than the average parent of high school students), his experience as both a parent and a high school coach, and his fluid honesty about his own children suggests that Larry believes his quote about the purpose of high school sports.

He offered his insights, furthermore, with a certainty reminiscent of the student athletes willing to speak on this topic—there was nothing awkward in his body language; he maintained eye contact, and his speech was consistent.

Larry is a teacher and a coach; therefore, he has an educator's perspective of high school sports to accompany what he believes as a father. Most parents obviously have no access to what Larry has been able to experience as both a father and a coach. His words about remembering the relationships more than the wins and losses appear to be authentic.

Both of Larry's sons experienced typical highs and lows associated with playing high school sports, and neither of his boys continued with competitive athletics at the college level. Perhaps most striking about Larry, however, was the sense of how difficult it was for him to remain calm in the face of all the potential high school sport conflicts. If it requires a great effort for a man like Larry to keep a level head, what happens to most of the parents?

Mark, an outspoken parent, offered the following: "From my standpoint, sports are about growing up and getting somebody in the right lane to grow up to be a positive adult. It gets you in the circle of good kids and good people and a good focus." These words are definitely in concert with both Larry's sentiments and the student athlete perspectives as well.

However, Mark provided opportunities to test these words against more of his words. If, in fact, the purpose of high school sports is to get children in a great circle of friends and give them positive direction, it is difficult to marry this view with, "Matt is a hard worker, a very smart student. . .but Matt's a klutz." Matt, it should be noted, is not Mark's son—and he was competing for playing time on a team with Mark's son.

Jane is a parent who has struggled with her identity as a mother within the high school sports arena. She has often removed herself from the presence of other adults during athletic competitions because of the discomforting words aimed at student athletes and coaches. It is not surprising, then, to hear Jane view the purpose of high school sports as "How to deal with others! Coaches, teammates, referees, parents, and the various perspectives on life." Although her words appear on paper to be directed toward student athletes, Jane was clear to point out that her purpose was for adults as well.

Do parents truly believe that high school sports are about getting kids "in the right lane to grow up to be a positive adult?" Is this reflected in their words and deeds when they are not sitting in front of an interviewer? There is nothing to suggest that the parents have intentionally lied to about their thoughts relating to high school sports. Mark most likely believes that high school sports should have a purpose to make his son a better person.

Asking parents about this topic and subsequently comparing their words with their behaviors (and the behaviors of thousands of other parents I observed), however, has provided a series of troubling notations of how parents have failed to identify a purpose for what gives them so much passion.

To begin, every parent interviewed on this topic—every one of them—has been covered in a nearly palpable sense of seriousness, even somberness, when discussing themselves, their own children, and everyone else associated with high school sports. What about the joy of high school sports? What about the carefree, restless spirit our youth can exercise by working with others at something as innocent as a sport?

This is not found in many parents today. They are worried about sports. They question their own behaviors and perhaps even feel guilt about their words and actions. They worry about their children. Are they too stressed about all of this? They worry about the coaches and principals and teachers and activities directors. Are these people doing the right things for their children?

One evening in early March a few years back, I found myself in a grocery store with two women, parents of girl basketball players at the school where I worked as a dean. They were standing together near the back of the store somewhere between the produce and the milk, and one of the women was visibly emotional while accepting the support of the other. To get to the milk, I needed to walk past these gals.

Knowing that they saw me, I walked over and asked if everything was alright. The woman with tears in her eyes thanked me and said, "They lost tonight. It's over." Her daughter's basketball team lost a tournament game a few hours beforehand (I was at the game). I tried to help the woman by reminding her that her daughter was a junior and there would be more games in the future. This was not helpful. I am thankful I had the wisdom to not say what I wanted to say.

With this, there are the actions of these parents. As dean of students, I supervised countless games throughout the school year. On one such occasion, I stood in the entryway of the gymnasium during a girls' basketball game so I could both watch the game and keep an eye on the commons area for wandering students. The girls were clearly outmatched on this night, and what I heard from the parents as they passed me at halftime was astounding.

One man, a father of one of the players, furiously looked me directly in the eyes and asked, "Why did I pay money for this bullshit?" Whatever the purpose for high school sports according to parents, their view appears to be clouded with a troublesome, obsessive passion.

The purpose of sport for a high school student athlete is not necessary shared by his or her parents. For example, not a single interviewed student athlete mentioned his or her talent compared to others in sports. On the contrary, every parent at least once referenced his or her son's or daughter's abilities in sports against other student athletes. The benefits of relationships are assumed for many adults; they participate for the potential exhilaration of competition.

EDUCATORS AND PURPOSE

What do school officials, including coaches and administrators, believe to be the purpose of high school sports? With this, does the philosophy of educators as it relates to a purpose for sports even matter anymore? Educators are stuck with the task of delivering a quality product of high school sports, and they find themselves trying to provide for the needs of the student athletes while appeasing the moms and dads (and usually the folks making all the noise are not capable of being pleased).

Somewhere after all of that work, educators can spend a moment deciding what they believe high school sports should accomplish. There is no mystery to the fact that high school sports have gotten messy. The problem for educators is simple and ironic: It does not matter what the mess of the moment is, or who is causing it. Educators will be blamed for it, and they are the only people capable of cleaning it up.

"All the things we need in life are taught in sports, if they are taught the right way." Roxanne, the source of this quote, has been a varsity coach in high school athletics for over twenty years. She, like many of the coaches and administrators interviewed, had no trouble at all discussing the purpose of high school sports.

Her mantra, "it's all about character," has led her to do what she believes is prudent despite the negatives (e.g., squabbles with parents, long hours, little pay) she painstakingly avoids discussing. There are many educators like Roxanne involved with sports. They show up, they get to work, and they try their best to ignore or forget some of the craziness going on around them.

Coaches like Roxanne often find a purpose, such as developing character, because they are working in a system (high school sports) that is consistently exposing young people to bad character. Roxanne must wonder, like many coaches, what happens at home when players return from a game to meet the dad who was angry enough to ask the dean of students why he paid money for this "bullshit."

When she was asked to elaborate on her need to teach character to young people, and whether she felt that her efforts have been hindered by other adults in the high school sports arena, Roxanne quickly dismissed the possibility of furthering the discussion. "I'm all about character with kids," was her answer. The discomfort she displayed while discussing her purpose for sports with the challenges provided by outside sources was obvious.

Mac, a veteran coach of several sports, offers another purpose for high school athletics. "I think it gives a student a chance to feel more involved in the school setting. They actually become a member of the school instead of someone simply attending the school. . .It is just a sense of belonging." Mac feels that high school sports, if done well, are priceless supplements to the educational process within schools.

These sports, he reasons, teach what is most difficult to teach. "Most jobs or occupations want someone who has team abilities or is able to work as a team member." In short, Mac offers that the purpose of high school sports for many, therefore, is to help fully realize the educational experience of the high school years.

Interestingly enough, Mac is considered by community members to be a very successful, winning coach. He has taken several teams, within more than a few sports, to state tournaments. Winning, however, is seldom breached with Mac when the purpose of high school sports is the topic. He is an educator first, the kind of man who would rather coach a bunch of lesser talented athletes who "get it" and work hard than a group of divas who win because they are physically gifted.

Educators celebrate coaches like Mac, but we do a terrible job selling his virtues to our public. There are many coaches of his ilk who struggle to get through a sports season without attending multiple conferences with the activities director, school board members, upset parents, and student athletes because of one conflict after another.

At the source, nearly all of these conferences stem from one of three realities: either the team is not winning enough, an individual player is not playing enough, or both.

Most people craft their concerns with more sophistication than actually admitting this; they claim the coach is favoring some kids over others, the coach yells too much, the coach is sending mixed messages, the list can go on and on. Coaches who win a great deal of their games, however, often have an amazing ability to somehow never favor some kids over others, yell too much, or send mixed messages—at least according to the public.

Our sport-crazy public has a difficult time understanding that in high school sports, winning and losing more than often boils down to the genetic make-up of a team's participants. For the most part, high schools cannot recruit its athletes. Any veteran coach can tell stories of the "once in a generation" teams they have seen regarding the good, the bad, and the ugly.

No one can coach five boys in a class of 100 to be 6'5, have cat-like reflexes, run like the wind, shoot the lights out, and jump out of the gym. Every once in a while, however, a coach inherits a team like this. And all veteran coaches know what else is inherited in bulk sometimes—a crew of short, slow, and very nice boys who all look more like Harry Potter than Lebron James.

So if winning and losing is so dependent upon that which is outside of a coach's control, what is a coach's role? What is the difference between good and bad coaches? Most educators closely affiliated with high school sports know these answers, yet again we fail to convey our wisdom to the public who so badly need to hear it. Coaches like Mac understand that their job in coaching is to do the best with what they have been given.

Clearly, great coaching can make differences on the scoreboard, especially when two teams with comparable talent are opposing each other. This is a minute aspect of high school coaching, however. Winning and losing in high school sports is usually a by-product of how things are done and how talented a team is compared to its opponent. For the most part, great coaches work with their student athletes to develop skills that have nothing to do with final scores.

This thought is echoed in the words of Gordon, a high school administrator who has spent his adult life around athletics. His views on purpose are as convincing as any. "I feel high school sports should be about perspective." Gordon believes that the purpose of high school sports should be to teach "perspective," but what is that? He explains that his years of coaching and mentoring have led him to believe that the best purpose for sports is to keep the activity fun and competitive while at the same time rational and educational.

"When I say 'perspective,' I mean that our coaches and our parents are keeping the activity in such a light that the experience is. . .about adults teaching (the student athletes) some of the skills that are necessary and not just emphasize win, win, win all the time." Gordon, it should be noted, is a member of the Minnesota Basketball Coaches Hall of Fame and has nearly 600 wins to his credit.

MIXED MESSAGES

On one hand, the problem is obvious. If kids, their parents, and educators are not viewing the purpose of high school sports as a whole, we are likely frequently disappointing one another with our words and actions. On the other hand, if the problem is that obvious we all would have developed a solution by now. The reality behind high school sports and how the different participants view its purpose is that strikingly few people, aside from great educators, are capable of removing "self" from their purpose equation.

Stories about great teachers, whether it is Mr. Jurgens in his psychology class or John Wooden with his college basketball teams, are ironically relevant to high school sports. Parents and community members may have dozens of philosophies between and among themselves about the purpose of school for children.

They may even feel strongly about what should be taught in English, history, or science classes. However, the vast majority of these adults also believe that their ideals are in no way developed enough, or important enough, to challenge the established practices of a school and its teachers.

And the critics of John Wooden's purpose? Their voices could have sooner been heard on Mars. By and large, outside sources do not interfere with the day-to-day events in a classroom. For better or for worse, our public either credits educators with knowing what needs to happen in the classroom—or they simply do not care enough to raise hell about it. With this reality, academia has little to fight regarding mixed messages.

This is not the case with high school sports. Whatever set of ideals parents and other concerned members of the community have about high school sports, they will be heard. Because of this—and only because of this—the presence of adults within high school sports has tremendous importance.

Why? Nearly every adult with a strong view of purpose for high school sports will in one way or another affect the kids playing. Further, the downside of these moms, dads, neighbors, and media folks caring this much about kids playing sports is not that they believe strongly about the purpose of sport. Rather, the downside is that no two people outside of kids and great educators, it seems, can agree on what the purpose should be. What does this do to high school student athletes?

One by-product of a conflicting purpose for high school sports can be seen in an unfortunate series of events ultimately leading to an immensely talented high school senior boy needing professional counseling to cope with a situation. The boy was simultaneously a fantastic student, a very talented athlete, and a gifted musician.

Remarkably, the young man found himself in a position to decide between participating and singing in an all-state choir function or playing in a hockey game scheduled for the same weekend. Considering he was a captain for his hockey team and highly skilled in the sport, many concerned onlookers were shocked when the boy hinted that he was leaning toward choosing the all-state choir experience over the sport.

The level of concern over this boy's decision was almost unbelievable. There were grown men and women, both educators and those outside of the school, who were using words like "traitor" and "soft" to describe a boy who was clearly struggling to do what he thought was best. Would he be letting his team down if he chose choir over hockey? Maybe. It is perhaps impossible, however, to fully grasp the many people, especially adults, who let him down during this stressful time.

The situation in which this boy found himself was the ultimate opportunity for wise adults, educators and otherwise, to teach. Instead, too many adults were choosing sides for the young man and trying to convince him to do what they thought was right. What was the right thing to do? Should a captain of the team lead by example and stay with the team? Clearly, the boy knew of his obligations to his teammates and coaches.

Should not a member of the choir be honored when given the opportunity to represent his school at an all-state concert and banquet? This boy, after all, earned this award; it was not a lottery which gave him this honor. Sometimes important things require a sacrifice, and sacrifice is not easy.

The drama associated with this high school senior boy and his decision to either play hockey or sing at all-state is a great example of how student athletes, educators, parents, and other community members cannot agree on a purpose for sports. Many of the people who referenced this boy as a traitor are the same people who would say that sports should be about getting kids "into the right lane." What is wrong about choosing all-state choir? How does that path lead to a stain upon the young man's resume?

Yes, there are decisions a senior high school boy could make that would be worthy of a raised eyebrow. Many student athletes choose, for example, to smoke pot and drink beer on weekends. When they are caught, these athletes miss games too. As an educator and coach, I have seen countless cases of student athletes making bad choices—drinking, smoking, vandalizing, etc...—and I have never seen any of these boys or girls suffer from their poor decisions at the hands of adults like the young man who, for one day, chose singing over a sport. It is difficult to comprehend that high school sports could have this purpose for anyone old enough to know better.

Because kids, their parents, members of the community, and educators cannot seem to agree on a purpose for high school sports, high school student athletes are often left confused, bitter, and regretful about their sport participation. Many student athletes manage to overcome the unavoidable negative influence and keep a healthy purpose for their participation. Others, unfortunately, begin to reflect the troubling expectations of the adults surrounding them.

WHO IS TO BLAME?

Who is at fault for the mess associated with high school sports? Is it those damn kids? They all have $100 cell phones now, and few of them have any idea how much work it takes to earn $100. They think they own the world and nothing should be as important as their fun. How about those crazy parents? These people run around like mad making sure their kids have everything they want, even if that means they get little of what they need.

After all, someone has to pay for those cell phones, right? How about all of us? Society is to blame because we have all been drinking the Kool-Aid and thinking that it is cute to worship teenagers for their athletic abilities. We have actually decided that the Little League World Series is something worthy of ESPN—we sit on the couch and watch twelve year-old kids we have never met play baseball. There are enough "crazies" to blame, right?

Specific suggestions are provided in the second half of this book; the first half (this chapter included) outlines the problems. Here is the problem in a nutshell regarding high school sports and purpose: participants of high school sports do not share a purpose for sports. Because of this, the kids are not benefiting from these sports as they should.

Blame? No one. Every one. Who cares. The only meaningful conclusion to be made about high school sports and purpose is that educators (administrators, coaches, teachers) have allowed all of these voices, both the wise and the crazies, time on stage.

THE PRICE

Crazy sport parents are not relieved of their parenthood when they make huge parenting mistakes. Educators, however, often do lose their jobs (or their minds) because of how people view sports. Great educators are the only people capable of keeping the crazies at bay, and we are not getting the job done. High school sports, therefore, is not worth what it should be worth for our young people.

Chapter Three

Relationship and Communication Quality

THE SIMPLE TRUTH

"They should just tell it like it is." These words came from a young man who had been soured by some of his high school sports experiences, especially from what he perceived as a difference between what adults said and what they intended. The boy, Wes, had not played on his basketball team as much as he hoped, and it caused strain between his coaches and his parents.

Wes admitted that these communication breakdowns had been realized, at times, despite the best intentions of those who care about him. "My mom thinks I'm a great basketball player, my dad thinks I'm a great basketball player, but I look at it like — they're my parents! Of course they're going to say that to me!"

The reality Wes needed verified by adults was simple: he was not a great basketball player, and there was no need to expect unrealistic greatness from him. Simply "telling it as it is" is difficult enough for many people, and that may not scratch the surface of the issues surrounding relationships and communication between and among school administrators, coaches, parents, and student athletes.

Relationship quality among high school personnel, student athletes, and parents is the strongest indicator for a successful or unsuccessful high school sports experience for everyone involved. Furthermore, the current state of relationship and communication quality between and among these groups is shameful.

SCHOOLS

Every public school district in our country prides itself on (or at least strives toward) fostering healthy relationships with the public, especially the students and their parents. Countless researchers have explained that children perform better in the classroom when their families are either involved in the process of education or they believe they are a great value to the school.

Many elementary schools, for example, value and depend upon strong parental involvement both during school hours and beyond. Volunteering is applauded in these schools; parents are revered for anything from assisting during arts and crafts time to their willingness to chaperone a field trip. Successful elementary schools are often viewed as those that develop and maintain a positive working relationship with its students and associated families.

The needs of elementary classrooms are much different than those of most high schools, however. High school math teachers have very little use for a parent to assist a classroom full of students with the balancing of equations. Furthermore, most high school teachers are quite thankful to have parents removed from the academic setting. Why? The relationship ideals between and among parents, students, and school personnel drastically change when the students are in high school.

An aggressively involved parent of a high school student, moreover, likely does much more to hinder the child in the high school years than to assist him or her. Any high school teacher could share what would happen if a parent walked into class and sat down next to his or her child to "help out" for the afternoon. It would be a nightmare for the student and likely the teacher. Appropriate parent involvement at the high school level happens in a respectful privacy, not for the world to see.

High school is a time of transition for students. It is expected of high school students that they grow in their independence, and for the most part the public reinforces this philosophy. Advanced placement courses are a great example of this. Courses like these are must-haves for many school districts; moms and dads want their sons and daughters to be prepared for success at the college level. Classroom settings like these are no place for parents.

Yes, there are still parent-teacher conferences in high schools. Yes, parents are still contacted when their child becomes a discipline problem within high schools. However, for the most part, there is an unwritten relationship rule for parents of high school students that they slowly back away and let their children experience an education for themselves.

And, surprisingly enough, almost all parents adhere to this relationship standard. Strikingly few parents of high school students meddle in the academic details of their child's schooling until and unless they are encouraged by the school to further their involvement. The argument could be made that too many parents have relinquished their duty to remain adequately and appropriately involved in their child's high school education because, if nothing else, their roles have become more passive. After all, high school kids do not need help in art class, they do not need a ride for the field trip, and most of them are not going to talk their parents' ears off about school at the end of the day.

Clearly, relationships matter in education, and the quality of communication between school district personnel and the public determines nearly every relationship conceivable. It is ironic, then, that the same parents who have gracefully granted independence in the academic arena for their high school aged sons and daughters have failed to deliver this gift where it is needed even more—in the world of sports.

Relationship and communication quality between and among school officials and the concerned public is far better when academics is concerned (even if that means a limited relationship with very little communication) than it is when high school sports are the focus. Why? Passion. As the first chapter of this book outlines, an alarming number of adults are more concerned about high school sports than they are about academics, character, work ethic, and reality.

Communicating with the public about sports has been made so vital for school officials that many schools provide up to three nights a year for parent-sport meetings, where the vast majority of the meeting is dedicated to clarify for parents what appropriate communication is and is not. Despite desperate attempts to cure many in the public of their poor relationship skills, school officials are suffering from the over-involvement of moms, dads, and other community members as these people try their best to enjoy high school sports.

There is a problem in our schools when academics are in the shadow of sports. The activities directors in most high schools are on the telephone with parents more than the principal and the teachers combined. There are more negative relationship issues associated with sports for school administrators to solve than any three topics aligned with academic successes or failures.

Graduation rate for our minorities going down? No biggie. A group of students receiving impressive academic scholarships for a major university? Maybe a paragraph in the local newspaper. The boys B-team basketball coach sits a player out of a game because of poor behavior in school? The telephone in the school office will ring itself right off the hook, and many of the calls are from people unrelated to the boy.

Not all relationships associated with schools are positive. Not all communication is open and honest. Not all parent and community involvement should be welcomed in school. High school sports have exposed some truths about what people care about and what they are willing to do or say in the name of their passions. This is not necessarily a reality created by school districts; however, it has been tolerated within our schools enough to damage our academic integrity, what we want our sports to represent, and the experience we hope to provide for our student athletes.

STUDENT ATHLETE PERSPECTIVES

"I'd rather have coaches be happy with me and be happy with the team than us win all the games in the world."

—Nick, High School Senior Athlete

These words from Nick were not spoken from the perspective of a student athlete struggling to find rays of hope within athletics. Nick did not see himself as a failure within athletics, he was not one who seldom attained playing time, and he was not, according to him, at odds with any of his coaches. What he projected, rather, was a refreshing bluntness. Nick offered a great perspective into high school sports, specifically his participation in hockey, by admitting that relationships are more important to him than winning and losing.

The friendships savored by high school athletes like Nick are often easily attained with other student athletes. The dynamics change, however, when school administrators, coaches, parents, and other concerned community members are inserted into the high school sports process. "There's no true friendships, I don't think, between coaches and parents." There is, of course, no way to prove a statement like this from Nick, but that is not the point.

Nick has been involved in youth sports long enough to notice the subtleties of relationships through the communication between and among school officials, coaches and parents, and what he has noticed has made him jaded toward many of the adults involved with high school sports. Nick is like most high school student athletes; he has resigned himself to believe that the school-parent relationship meet only one criteria: "Whatever they do is fine, if it doesn't ruin it for me."

What kind of relationships should adults display, according to student athletes? Christine, a senior athlete when interviewed, emphasized the role of an ideal adult in high school sports by detailing their need to stay out of the way. "I do it (participate in sports) for the people more than anything. Basketball's not my favorite sport, but I do it for the girls."

Christine clearly expressed what it was she gained from high school sport participation, and her values were heavily reliant upon solid, positive relationships with people aligned with her through these sports. "But I have heard some situations where there's a lot of pressure on some girls when they go home, and that's just so stupid. . .That just brings the whole team morale down."

This perspective is interesting and indicative of the bigger picture sought within this book. Christine described relationships between other student athletes and their parents and how their relationships affected more than just their own families. She had often seen the damage caused by inconsistent and conflicting communication.

When parents say one thing to a student athlete, and school personnel say another, the student athlete is likely in an awkward position. "They (student athletes) come to practices and games and they've kind of got this idea of, 'Hey, I'm pretty good. . .Why aren't I playing more?'"

The problems stemming from poor relationship and communication skills are often far more pressing than a kid wondering why he or she is not granted more playing time. High school athletes are adolescents, and whether it seems like it or not, they are learning how to behave by watching the adults in their lives handle relationships. What these adolescents are learning is sometimes worthy of great pause.

As a dean of students, I was often in a position to witness people at a crossroads. Students, for example, are frequently faced with an opportunity in school to correct a mistake. More often than not, a student's misstep in a school setting will result in an adult educator's guidance to improve and correct the student's behavior—and the student will do just that. The building of relationship and communication skills is a daily occurrence in any high school setting. Teaching decency and good character through high school sports, however, is often a great challenge for leaders in education.

One such challenge came in the form of a high school hockey player and his family. The player, a junior, was removed from a game by a referee for an illegal hit on an opposing player (he hit him from behind into the boards). Unfortunately, these things happen in high school sports—especially in contact sports. However, the behaviors and actions resulting from this situation are far more revealing than the incident itself.

The player, based on state high school league rules, was suspended for one game for his illegal hit. He met with the school's activities director, the head hockey coach, and me, and it was suggested to him that it would be a display of great sportsmanship to write a letter to the opposing player, a boy who had received a concussion because of the hit, apologizing and checking on his health status. The boy agreed with us and expressed both a concern for the player he hurt and a willingness to cooperate.

One day later, the suspended player's mother delivered a letter to high school administrators and hockey coaching staff explaining that her son will "not write such a letter" unless, of course, her son also receives apology letters from every athlete who has hurt him over the years. At this point, the activities director scheduled a meeting with the boy and his parents. Hoping to find some common ground, the activities director and I believed that there must have been some simple breakdowns in communication and that the situation could be easily corrected. We were naïve.

Other than my presence, the meeting was attended by the activities director, the head hockey coach, the boy, the boy's two parents, and an attorney for the boy's family. It should be noted that, other than the state high school penalty, the suspended player faced no punishment. Our administration staff and hockey coaches determined that his actions on the ice were a result of competitive aggression and that he had no intention to injure the opposing player.

The suggestion to write a letter to the boy he injured was offered as an act of decency, something good people do when they have the opportunity. This was made very clear to the boy when we met with him. It is unclear whether the boy communicated this to his parents or not, but it was made strikingly clear to everyone affiliated with our school district that the lawyer was brought to the meeting to protect the boy from any further punishments.

During the meeting, the activities director offered to the family and their attorney that sometimes people can apologize for a situation, even if they do not feel they were at fault for anything—much like apologizing to someone when a loved one dies. Sometimes, the activities director implored, we can be sorry because we simply regret an outcome. The parents refused to allow their son to apologize. They also refused to shake hands with any of the administrators or coaches when they left the meeting.

Who is the most important person in the story above? Without question, it is the boy. What did the young man learn from these events involving hurting someone (intentionally or not) and demonstrating responsibility? The entirety of this story centers on the power of effective (or completely ineffective) communication and healthy (or incredibly unhealthy) relationships associated with the high school sports experience.

If it is important to Nick that he get along with his coaches and teammates, and if Christine plays high school sports "for the people, more than anything," then for what reasons do the parents of the young man (who was merely asked to write a letter) participate? More importantly, what is it they are teaching their son?

When life-lessons need to be taught in the classrooms and hallways of high schools, great teachers and administrators feel an obligation to teach. Furthermore, the lessons are learned. Why? There are no middle-men involved in the classrooms, at least not like there are where sports are involved.

Communication in schools is effective when the educators are both wise and willing to do or say the right things to young people for the right reasons. Ironically, these educator-student relationships are valued and trusted by many of the same parents who either cannot or will not remove themselves from the equation when high school sports are involved. This is not what students want from the adults in their lives. More importantly, it is not what they need.

Parent and Community Member Perspectives

> "I always said, 'Oh, you'll be a football player!' But it was the group of kids that he got to know and be close to, so he played soccer. That group was important to him and soccer was secondary."
> —Chris, Parent of Senior in High School

Two pieces of truth are evident from Chris' words above. First, parents like Chris (and recent high school sports realities suggest that she is not uncommon) have their own hopes and desires for the athletic careers of their children. Second, parents are at least on some level aware that relationship quality is an important—if not, the most important—piece of the high school sports experience for their children.

Soccer is not a game Chris understands or truly enjoys; she did little to hide this when she spoke. She was eager, furthermore, to offer the truth that she "allowed" her son to choose this sport because of his desire to maintain great relationships with his friends who also played soccer. Chris, it should be noted, was an outstanding high school athlete. Specifically, she excelled in basketball.

It is interesting that Chris, when discussing her son's relationship with the varsity soccer coach, regarding a sport about which she knows very little, can claim, "We (her husband and she) are not going to call the coach and ask why. If he (her son) is not satisfied, then it's his job to advocate for himself." She added that her job was to help support the coach and not talk about any differences (between the coach and herself) in front of her son.

Regarding basketball, a sport she knows well, however, the message from Chris altered enough to take notice. Although she did not recant the need for her children to advocate for themselves (more than one of her children played high school basketball at the time of her interview), it was not emphasized. When speaking about the participation of her children in high school basketball, Chris' very first words were these: "We want to win. We want to win when we are on varsity." We?

Mark, a parent of several high school athletes when interviewed, was quick to remind that his role as a parent of student athletes diminished greatly as his children progressed into high school. "I'm a firm believe that parents can only do so much." Not a man to avoid the topic or use subtleties when straight-talk will suffice, Mark acknowledged the reality of conflict among high school sport participants.

Student athletes, their parents, high school administrators, and coaches are not always going to see eye-to-eye, and Mark claimed that is not necessarily a negative for his children. "I think it's good for a child to develop the youth-adult conversation skill. It is out of their comfort level, but it's a part of growing up. You have to do things that are out of your comfort level."

There is no reason to doubt Mark believes what he said about student athletes benefiting from developing communication skills with adults. However, it is doubtful that Mark believes all coaches are worthy of his restraint from speaking either to them or about them as coaches. When speaking about the current basketball coach of his son, for example, Mark offered, "I didn't think (he) should have been a head coach. . .I just don't think he has the personality to deal with kids at this age. . .that sent our basketball program back so far."

Parents appear to know how important positive relationships are for their children to truly enjoy high school sports. They also seem to agree, at least in their conversations, it is best for their children if parents are as removed as possible with the process of conflict resolution between school officials and student athletes.

As Keith, a parent of two heavily involved student athletes, stated, "It's not the parent's job to go in there and threaten the coach, play the 'political' card, or whatever. . .If parents want to be over-involved and start coaching from the sideline or their kitchen table, then they need to be a coach and start volunteering then."

Darlene, a parent of two high school student athletes, however, reminds that knowing as a parent that positive communication and harmonious relationships are necessary for the success of student athletes is akin to a cigarette smoker knowing that quitting that terrible habit is what is best for his or her health. "Your first instinct is if your kid is hurting from sports, you want to protect him." Knowing the right thing and doing the right thing are clearly two different tasks for parents.

There is a reality with parents and some members of the community as they work to participate within the relationships of high school sports. The relationship they have is with their child, or with certain children for whom they care, and everyone else involved are merely people with common interests.

Things can go along smoothly for quite a while with this line of thinking; sometimes serious conflicts are avoidable. However, when conflict does occur in high school sports between either themselves or their child and anyone else involved within the common interest (coaches, administration, other parents, other players, etc. . .), there is little doubt about where allegiances will lie.

Two interviewed parents admitted this truth. Darlene emphasized that "every parent, EVERY parent thinks that their kid has talent!" Mark added that "every parent is lying if they say they don't have rose colored glasses. You (the parent) just don't see things fair and (im)partial." Unfortunately, this is not often the perspective student athletes need or want from their parents. And it is almost never the perspective educators need or want from parents.

Two experiences from my years as a dean of students perfectly paint the picture of relationship and communication conflict as it relates to parents of high school student athletes. The first is from an event many school districts conduct at least once a year, a parent-sport meeting. The second involves the first game of the season for a boys basketball team, and it is especially interesting and revealing considering it happened within a week of the parent-sport meeting.

The parent-sport meeting consisted of the school district's activities director consistently and carefully sharing essential information for sport participation with both student athletes and, more importantly, their parents. Aside from a few house-keeping issues, the bulk of the presentation revolved around the importance of demonstrating appropriate communication and relationship skills as parents. The following topics were the first five covered in the meeting:

1. Communication—adults were urged to act like adults. This, the activities director explained, begins with how we treat each other and how we communicate with one another.
2. Appropriate concerns to discuss with a coach—parents were told it is not acceptable to contact a coach about playing time. They can contact a coach about grades, health issues, etc. . .but not playing time.
3. Conflict resolution—here are the rules for when participants have problems. . .First, the student athlete needs to talk to the coach. Then, the student athlete and the parent should talk to the coach together. Only after that can the student athlete, the parent, the coach, and the activities director meet. Parents should never call a school board member with a conflict.
4. Pro athletes versus high school athletes—high school sports is not a "win at all costs" enterprise.
5. True purpose of sports—high school sports is about character building, developing work ethic, learning to win, learning to lose, building relationship skills, establishing friendships, etc. . .

The meeting lasted about forty-five minutes, and one with an outsider's perspective would likely think that it was a success. None of the ideas were received by parents with controversy. In fact, most parents could be seen nodding their heads and agreeing with the necessity of the topics being presented. There was a jovial, stress-free look on most of the faces that evening. The problems discussed at the meeting? Those are "other" people acting crazy. The rules set forth by the school? Those will only be necessary for those "others."

Emotions are at their lowest before a sports season begins (this meeting was a few days before the winter season). However, when conflicts arise, all which is covered in a parent-sport meeting will be forgotten and ignored in an instant. The entire meeting, as it is in every high school, was a great idea. It was falling on many deaf ears.

How do we know this? Because less than a week later a parent who attended that meeting violated nearly every rule covered in the parent-sport meeting and invented a few violations of his own in the process. During half-time of the first game of the boys basketball season, an irate father confronted the activities director and questioned him about the playing time of his son during the first half. Note: The season, at this point, was twenty minutes old. The parent was making a scene so disturbing that it forced the activities director to remove the man from view and into the administration office.

As it turned out, the student athlete involved with this story (the boy who supposedly did not play enough in the first half of the first game) had a meeting with his coach and the activities director the next morning to discuss the events of the night before. The young man cried throughout the entire meeting and made the following contributions: First, he wanted to know what he could do to play more. Next, he begged the basketball coach to not hold him accountable for the behavior of his father.

People like the father in this brief story are recognized by everyone associated with high school sports. Everyone knows "that guy" who is stupid about sports, his kids, and the combination of the two. "Some people" get carried away, "some parents" cannot keep their emotions under control. It is interesting, however, that when given the opportunity to step forward and assist high school coaches and administrators by either counseling these crazy parents into sanity or informing them that their tactics are inappropriate, very few parents are capable of stepping forward.

This is tragically ironic for everyone involved with high school sports because even the best parents have children who are negatively affected by "that guy" being crazy about sports. Furthermore, absolutely no one in today's world, even the nicest and most patient parents of any community, would tolerate this brand of craziness from a coach or an administrator without raising hell beyond recognition.

The problem for schools and crazy sport parents is clear: whether it is a teacher's or coach's or an administrator's fault or not, the communication and relationship mess is left for educators to clean.

EDUCATOR PERSPECTIVES

"One of the things that I've studied over the years is that kids truly hate driving home with their parents after a game and having the whole game critiqued."
—Gordon, High School Administrator and Hall of Fame Coach

Most high school coaches discuss their roles as communicators much in the same light high school guidance counselors describe their jobs. These coaches, if they are at all good at what they do, are required to be emotional custodians, cleaning up one ugly incident after another while trying to both protect individual student athletes and advance entire teams.

Parents, Gordon reminds, take home only one piece of that team puzzle every night; coaches are asked to use and make sense of every piece every day. "You have tunnel vision many times when it comes to your own kid," Gordon admits. But many parents have proven to Gordon, a Hall of Fame coach with over thirty years experience, that they are at least capable of "willing to trust the expertise of coaches."

How can parents, student athletes, and high school administrators and coaches coexist and trust the relationships structured within high school sports? Perhaps, Gordon, suggests, it begins with something small, yet simple, regarding how we model our communication. "There's not a kid around who will say they really like when their parents scream at the coaches, the officials, or the other team. . .That is embarrassing for the kid."

Mac, a great veteran teacher and coach, explains that coaches are obligated to communicate, as much as possible, these realities so that potential distractions caused by strained relationships can be avoided. "I think once kids understand what their strengths are and what their weaknesses are, and then if parents understand that as well, then everyone knows why the kids is playing in the position he or she is in."

Lloyd, a head coach of two varsity sports, understands and agrees with the duty to communicate as Mac describes; however, his experiences have trained him to be wary of relationships involving parents of athletes he is coaching. Effective communication with many in the public, therefore, has become a balancing act between friendly, inviting small-talk and cold, un-emotional business.

Lloyd points out, and Mac certainly understands this as well, that building and maintaining effective relationships with student athletes and especially their parents is fine as long as some parents are never told "truths" they do not want to hear.

During a volleyball game Lloyd was coaching, one parent was overheard by Lloyd (and half of Lloyd's hometown) yelling, "She needs to get a cork out of her ass and start moving!" The parent, Lloyd later learned, was referring to a girl competing for a position against this parent's daughter. Lloyd shared that even in the present day, months after that embarrassing event happened, there was still a source of great discomfort for many of the student athletes participating on his team.

And who is charged with mending those fences? Things like this are more common in sports than anyone outside of education would care to imagine. What communication and/or relationship skill would Lloyd have needed to prevent that parent from yelling those hateful words?

Student athletes, parents, and, perhaps even to a greater extent, educators are fully aware of the significance of effectively communicating and maintaining positive relationships among themselves. To a large degree, however, educators, unlike anyone else involved in high school sports, are often viewed as responsible for the effectiveness of these relationships.

Jack, a veteran hockey coach, pointed out a truth with which few associated with high school sports can argue. "No mothers or fathers ever get fired, nor do they every get nasty anonymous letters, for speaking their mind whenever and however they wish to speak—and no one holds them accountable when their words are proven to be wrong."

Part of my duties as a dean of students required that I supervise sporting events. My responsibilities during games and matches ranged from providing necessities for referees, ensuring the student body was displaying appropriate fan behavior, and for many events I was charged with transporting money collected at the door to the bank. By and large, however, my most important task was to be seen by both the student body and their parents.

Many concerned with high school sports badly want to know that somebody from the high school other than coaches and student athletes care about these events. My presence at these games, furthermore, produced many opportunities to observe high school sports occurrences I could have never fathomed otherwise.

One of these events was at a girls soccer match. The evening of this match was unbelievably cold and wet; those who stood outside to watch the game that evening were dressed like the King Crab fishermen off the Bering Sea. Both the boys and girls soccer programs used a portable, generator-run, electronic scoreboard. The equipment, both the scoreboard and the remote for it, were fickle even in the best of weather.

Needless to say, I had my worries about overseeing an electronic scoreboard while rain seemed to be coming from directions physics could not explain. In short, as the high school administrator on site, I elected to house the electronic equipment so that it would not be damaged, and, more importantly, no one (me) would somehow be electrocuted from it. What followed this decision was nothing short of amazing.

"Hey, what's the score?" a dad asked. This man, like everyone else suffering through this experience, knew the score. We had been out in the pasture our school district called a soccer field for over two hours and no one had even come close to scoring a goal yet.

"Will the scoreboard be working for the boys games?" This bit of sarcasm was insinuation that the scoreboard was removed because of the gender of the players. Somehow, despite sideways rain, temperatures below forty degrees, and a school district that permitted student athletes to compete in weather than could have caused serious injuries, this particular mother voiced her displeasure with the school district's sexism.

"Will the football team play without a scoreboard this week?" This accusation included both gender and sport discrimination as a weapon. There were, of course, plenty of parents who said nothing, but the remarks of the few who did comment made me pause.

I said nothing, absolutely nothing, to these parents. It was pouring down rain. It was freezing cold. I truly believe the scoreboard would have been damaged. I was truly worried I would have been zapped. I was seriously considering calling the game off because of the weather conditions, these idiots were concerned with a scoreboard, and I said nothing. I regret my silence to this day.

Later that year I supervised a basketball game; it was a Friday night and the gymnasium was filled with student body, parents of players, and community members. Like most of my supervising in the gymnasium, I positioned myself in the doorway of the gym so I could see and hear the student body, the game, and the commons area. The home team lost badly that night, and I was in a position to hear things I still cannot comprehend.

"This is embarrassing!" These words came from a father of one of the boys playing.

"What the hell is he (the coach, I assume) doing?"

"You tell me. . .give me one reason why he (a player) is on the floor!" This was a woman I did not recognize, but she was pointing at a boy from our school and loud enough for several rows of people to hear.

"Why did I pay money for this shit?" This last question was directed at me. I stared at the man who asked this, not out of anger—I was too shocked to be mad. I remember him looking back at me, with rage in his eyes; he was seriously angry. With as much wit as I could muster, I stared him down and answered, "I have no idea, sir, but I can get you a refund if you need to go cool off somewhere..." It was halftime. He said nothing else the rest of the game.

This middle-ground educators find themselves in is actually part of the problem as it relates to the relationships in high school sports. Sometime over the past few years, it has become expected of teachers, administrators, and coaches to turn the other cheek away from the crazies, while at the same time teaching and coaching, while at the same time shielding the youth from the crazies we dare not address.

It is enough to make one's head spin. At the same time, we are forced to overcome ourselves. This can be seen with a volleyball coach, for example, screaming the words "You have to have self control out there!" so loudly and in such barbaric fashion that his voice literally hit falsetto by the end of the sentence.

What if it would have been a group of students sarcastically asking about the scoreboard and whether or not it would be used for the boys game or the football game? Everything would have stopped, right there and right then, and they would have made to feel foolish for their selfishness. Ironically, not a single student watching the soccer game said a word about the scoreboard.

Why would they? Those who were there were trying to stay warm by huddling together and drinking hot cocoa, and they knew that there had been no goals scored all evening. And how about the athletes and coaches, did they notice? No, they were playing the game, and they too knew the score.

It takes adults to screw up relationships via their communication when it comes to high school sports. This book was born the night of that soccer game, the night a series of inconsiderate people dared to question my decency and I allowed them to do it without so much as saying a word to them. That night was the last I ever let myself be meek in the face of the crazies.

I decided that not because I have a necessity to be macho; I am clearly not easily confrontational. Rather, I have become vocal about what I know is right and wrong because I am an educator, and these people are hurting my progress with students.

Too many good people, educators and community members alike, sit silent and let crazy sport parents (and, unfortunately, sometimes even educators) do and say whatever they want, regardless of their impact. Unfortunately, theirs are the relationship skills that are killing our sports programs.

WHOSE FAULT IS IT?

The quality of communication and relationships in high school sports is at its lowest point. Kids know that they need both each other and the relationships they have with adults, yet they find themselves admitting that they hope their parents, other parents, coaches, and administrators somehow stay out of their way enough to keep sports fun.

Parents either know that problems exist with the way some of their own handle high school sports—and if they do not, the chances are good that they are the problem. However, this does little to change poor behavior when it happens. Mr. and Mrs. Jones do not believe it is their job to make sure that Mr. and Mrs. Johnson behave at a football game.

Educators are in the best (or worst) seat in the house. They are charged with teaching and coaching students, and with that responsibility comes daily communication and relationship skills with both students and their families. With that, they are the filters in the high school sports process. Who controls the message? Who decides the relationships? Because Mr. and Mrs. Jones are not willing to address Mr. and Mrs. Johnson, and student athletes are not capable of it, the job falls to educators. The problem is, educational leaders are not doing it.

The conflicting messages between the parents and the school officials must have been nearly paralyzing for the hockey player who was asked to write a letter to the boy he hurt. It is difficult to imagine what the "scoreboard parents" at the soccer game remembered about that night. When they discussed the game with their daughters, what was their focus? And how about the father who wondered aloud why he paid money "for this shit?" What did his son hear from him about the game? What if that boy played as well as he could that night and the other team was just that much better?

And how about the coaches we can find seemingly everywhere who sound like their head is going to explode during a game? Can these coaches look at their own children after such screaming and histrionics without feeling ashamed?

Right, wrong, and whom to blame is irrelevant when it comes to high school kids, parents, and school officials dealing with the issue of maintaining good working relationships. If students are pulled in two different directions, responsible for fulfilling both the wishes of their parents and the expectations of their coaches and school officials, then the adults in their lives are failing them.

Chapter Four

Success

NARCISSISM

Narcissus, a mythical, ancient Greek character, was renowned for his incredible beauty. A terrific athlete, he was deeply proud—often to the point of pushing aside those who loved him, preferring instead to focus on himself and his greatness. His rival, Nemesis, knew of Narcissus' self love, and used it against him.

Nemesis led Narcissus to a clear pool, where he could see his own beautiful reflection. Not realizing that the image he adored was nothing more than a self-loving temptation, Narcissus was unable to leave the poolside, eventually falling into the water and drowning.

High school sports have become a breeding ground for narcissism among our adolescent student athletes. At its core, youth sports are being wounded by self love and a lost perspective. Student athletes, especially boys, can be found in any school believing they have accomplished incredible feats. Further, many of these kids now believe their lives as high school athletes are far more important than their own academic success, the well-being and success of classmates, teammates, and peers, and the lives of their own family members.

In reality, the vast majority of these student athletes are average at best. An alarming number of high school athletes, however, have the ego of Michael Jordan and enough skill to be a role player on a college intramural squad.

Is there any mystery as to how this trend happened? If high school student athletes believe their sporting lives are more important than the lives of their moms, dads, and anyone else, it is likely because that belief has become a reality.

Adolescent athletes have somehow dictated when mothers and fathers can take vacations, when and if supper will be served on schedule, what kind of vehicle the family must drive (sports equipment takes up space), and whether or not happiness is allowed for a twenty-four-hour period after every game.

Many of these student athletes actually believe they will receive a scholarship to play college sports while at the same time being too short, too slow, and too uncoordinated to be a good player on their high school varsity team. And while all this is happening, the stuff these kids should be focused on regarding college—studying, for example—is being profoundly neglected.

The amazing part about narcissism in high school sports is not that there are student athletes who have grandiose perceptions of themselves, but rather the fact that more of them do not. Adolescents have an incredible ability to keep their peers grounded, and this is exactly why many, if not most high school athletes are more humbled and realistic among their peers than they are with members of their family and educators. Further, the trend of being an adolescent superstar in one's own home is relatively new. In the not-too-distant past, moms and dads were not in the habit of anointing their adolescent sons and daughters as high school athlete royalty.

I remember riding in the passenger seat of my dad's car as an eighth grader. I was talking to him about my basketball team, and the one-sided conversation eventually drifted toward my criticisms and suggestions for both teammates and our coach. My dad listened for quite a while before finally responding to my sports bantering. We stopped at a red light, and he turned to me with a completely blank face and said, "Son, you're just not good enough to talk like this."

I was floored—and it was the best thing he could have ever said to me at that moment. Needless to say, my parents were never awestruck in the wake of my high school athletic accomplishments, nor was our family's sense of identity defined by my sports schedule. My parents were too busy to worship me, and I am better now because of it. Not enough moms and dads today are willing to use truth to teach humility.

Although perhaps not as guilty as moms and dads in creating a generation of over-indulged student athletes, educators, nonetheless, are not off the hook. What we in education are willing to do or say in the name of sports is astounding. This was pointed out beautifully years ago by a senior girl in my English class. That year, as it turned out, a few teams and several individual student athletes competed in the state tournament. Before any of these teams or individuals left for "state," our school conducted a pep-rally for them in the gymnasium.

By the end of the school year, by the time some kids on the track team left for state, our pep-rallies were seriously lacking some pep. However, because we did not dare offend any of these athletes and their parents, we kept the pep-rallies coming.

It became embarrassing for all of us, but in the name of fairness, we made ourselves look like fools in front of high school kids that knew better. The girl in my English class informed me very late in the school year that she was attending some all-state band functions over the summer break.

After we spoke about it for a minute, she sarcastically wondered if I could pull together the faculty, student body, and pep-band for one more totally awesome rally in the gym. Jokes aside, her point was made. Educators have often made being a successful high school athlete akin to being famous.

This does not help us in education when we need our students to understand that successes and failures in high school sports are at best temporary and that real success is the result of using these experiences as stepping stones into adult life.

High school kids, if coached and parented well, will play sports for the right reasons. They will cherish the relationships they have established, and they will grow to comprehend the reality of their talents and their relative insignificance (as athletes) to the world as a whole. If kids are coached and parented well, they will see sports as a backdrop, a wonderful expression of passion. But all too often this is not being provided for high school student athletes.

Character building, truth telling, and establishing good relationships are fantastic in the eyes of many parents and some educators, as long as the people they care about are not doing the heavy lifting. For too many people, their perceptions of success in high school sports have regressed so far away from reality that they are in danger of drowning in their own clear pool.

GOOD COACH/BAD COACH

It is almost impossible for some people who feel a passion for high school sports to look beyond winning and losing. Coaches, furthermore, are often the only people to "blame" for losing games. Three interviewed parents, for example, described coaches who they perceived as unsuccessful.

In every situation, the evaluated coaches lost far more games than was expected (or tolerated) by these parents. These parents shared that traits like team morale and positive motivation were significantly lacking from the team; moreover, according to these folks, the coaches were responsible for what was missing—and responsible for the lack of fun provided for their children.

These three parents were describing three different coaches, and each coach was believed to be significantly deficient in coaching ability. No parent has ever spoken to me about a coach with a winning record who fails at building team morale, however. It would appear that coaches who win most of their games are not examined as closely by parents as those who lose most games. Or, it would appear that coaches who win most of their games have very little issue with building team morale or motivating student athletes.

In reality, high school coaches know the ugly truth about winning and losing: very few people want to admit that winning means as much as it does, so these people dance around the truth with issues like team morale and positive motivation. Amazingly, they are also given a platform to complain about it in front of our administrators almost any time they want.

When the concerned public hitches their collective wagons to winning and losing more than anything else, even if they will not admit they are doing it, high school sports become an awful mess. Three truths must be recognized both in our school districts and subsequently in the homes within our communities: First, good coaches can lose many games. How and why? Sometimes the opponents are better, sometimes the group of athletes he or she are hired to coach are not very athletic, and sometimes weird things happen in high school sports. Second, bad coaches can win many games.

Yes, there are men and women coaching high school sports who are not serving our children, our schools, and our communities as well as they should be. How do they win so much? Sometimes opponents are worse, sometimes the group of students he or she are hired to coach are incredibly athletic, and sometimes weird things happen in high school sports. Third, losing is not fun. It is difficult to keep high school athletes uplifted and motivated when they seldom win games.

Mac, a successful veteran teacher and coach, spoke at length about the difficulties many parents of athletes have defining a successful high school sports experience. The following words were shared with me at the conclusion of our conversation; his voice was filled with passion as though he was hoping somehow what he was saying could be heard by those who need to hear it:

> *When I talk with parents about issues in high school sports. . .How minor and insignificant those things are compared to the whole scope of things! Their kids are healthy, intelligent, athletic people. If they had known ahead of time, when they were going to give birth, they would have been the happiest parents in the world. But somewhere along the line, that wasn't good enough. . .*
> *Your kid is not going to be a professional athlete! Chances are, they're not even going to be a college athlete! Enjoy it for what it is; having fun, spending time with their friends, getting a great experience out of it. Don't get caught up with all the playing time issues. Because, to tell you the truth, to most kids, that is not the big issue with them.*
> *I ask kids the question: "Hey, what do you enjoy about sports the most?" I'm thinking they're gonna say, "going to state" or "when we won twenty-six games." No, they tell me that their favorite part is the bus rides! Every single*

kid, without exceptions. The bus rides! Staying overnight in a hotel! Interact-
ing with the team! Wins and losses were nothing. Playing time is not even in
their top five of priorities.
I wish parents would understand that when it's all said and done, that it's not
going to come down to those little nit-picky issues. It's going to come down to
the experience your son or daughter had playing sports.

This coach has perfectly detailed the tremendous gap between what student athletes see and what many of their parents and some in education see as it relates to high school sports. Student athletes, their parents, and educators do not share a meaning for a successful high school sports experience.

The joys and challenges of competition are an assumption for student athletes; they participate for the benefit of sharing their passions with friends. On the other hand, many adults, educators included, assume the benefits of positive relationships in sport participation; they participate for the competition.

THE NEED FOR STUDENTS TO COMPARE

What is success for adolescents playing sports? Of course high school athletes want to win games. Of course high school athletes want to compete, to be better than their opponent, to be an impressive member of their team. This is undeniable. Many high school athletes, furthermore, know exactly how they stack up against their competition. But adolescents play high school sports for other brands of success as well. High school student athletes use sports as a backdrop to accomplish what they really want.

As a dean of students, I spent over two hours a day supervising high school students as they ate lunch. It was during this time that I heard, and at times participated in, some of the best conversations imaginable. One conversation I overheard involved a table-full of six varsity boy hockey players. It was a game day for these boys, and they were scheduled to leave school within an hour. They were dressed up, they were smiling, they were laughing, and they were willing to share some of their thoughts with me.

I asked them who they were playing that night, and they answered with a six-man concert—"Roseau." I knew what that meant, and, obviously, they knew too. The boys continued to smile and laugh about the evening ahead of them, and they were completely honest about their prospects.

"So. . .how good is Roseau?" I asked. I knew the answer.

"They're as good as they always are," came from one boy who spoke above the noise of laughter from the others. Roseau Hockey, it should be noted, is renowned for its excellence—that is, the Roseau Rams win a ton of hockey games and quite often represent their section in the state tournament.

"Can you beat 'em?" I furthered. There was an amazing pause from the boys. They looked at me and smiled. Every one of us knew the truth; these boys were not going to beat the Roseau Rams. I sought words to transition from what I perceived as discomfort coming from the boys. Before I could speak, one of the boys, a senior, broke the silence.

"It's no big deal, Mr. Tufte, we know we're not gonna win." This was my opportunity.

"And that's ok, isn't it?"

We all spoke for a while about playing games against great opponents, winning some, losing some, and what matters. The conversation between the six hockey players and me was a moment better than I could have ever wanted. It is quite possible that tater tots and fruit cups were flying about the cafeteria while I was ignoring the bulk of the student body, but it was worth it. As the conversation waned and I began to once again notice the rest of the lunch-goers, one of the hockey players perfectly concluded our chat.

"You know what we were laughing at when you walked over here? We were talking about what kind of sub we're getting after the game. . .Every time we go to Roseau, we get to stop at Subway on the way home. . ."

Any coach who has ever given a less than truthful motivational speech to his or her players knows that high school athletes are fantastic at detecting B.S. Looking into the eyes of high school kids who are down by thirty-five points at halftime and saying, "We are still in this thing, guys!" is the equivalent of a schoolyard bully saying "I'm sorry" as he punches one of his victims.

High school athletes know the truth about talent, and they know that their coaches know the truth. When does a thirty-five point halftime deficit become a victory? Never, if victory is only found on the scoreboard. When we are down thirty-five points at halftime, we are not "still in this thing"—unless, of course, we all realize that we play sports for reasons beyond the scoreboard.

At the very core of high school sports, when all the fear and political correctness is removed from the words of student athletes, they will tell anyone willing to listen what success is. Most high school athletes, whether they are acting like a diva at home or not, have already finished comparing themselves to their teammates and opponents.

They know the truth about their abilities, and many of them have concluded that playing as hard as they can and having a tasty sandwich after the game is a pretty good way to spend a Friday.

THE NEED FOR ADULTS TO COMPARE

The need to compare their children to other kids happens naturally for most parents, and it begins well before their children even know what sports are. Educators are also naturally guilty of this necessity. Whether we are working with student athletes in a gymnasium, a rink, or on a field, or surviving a curriculum mapping committee meeting, we in education have become enamored in the quest of measuring students and, more importantly, ourselves.

How are we doing compared to China? How are we doing compared to the high school across town? What is our AYP status? What is our record in the conference? Will this finally be the year we beat North High?

Day care and preschool providers now have conferences with parents about the abilities and school readiness of their children. Issues like social skills, hygiene habits, and a willingness to quietly rest at nap time are balanced with the various developmental, intellectual goals established for children too young for public school.

Somehow there has become an established norm for four-year-old behavior at a preschool; many of these facilities have checklists for acceptable behaviors and outcomes. Johnnie plays well with others—check! Johnnie is willing to clean up toys after play-time—check! Johnnie will rest without disturbing others—no check!

Without fail, even children at this stage of life are compared to other children. Why? Have school districts ever held a kid back until he was nine years-old because he did not share well at preschool? No, it is because Johnnie's parents want to know if other kids are as socially fantastic and responsible as Johnnie and if any other kids are struggling at nap time too. If so, maybe the preschool should end nap time.

When comparisons are made this early in the education process, it is understandable how the situation can become out of hand by the time these children are high school students. Great high school teachers can tell countless stories from their parent-teacher conferences. It is common for parents of high school upperclassmen, for example, to bring a competitive edge to a conference.

It is often not enough for moms and dads to hear that their child is handling the Shakespeare unit nicely or that they appear to be comprehending pre-Calculus reasonably well. Rather, parents who have maintained a commitment to attending parent-teacher conferences for the duration of their child's school career (and these people are rare) want to know how their kid stacks up against the others.

Educators have done very little to subdue these urges. We glorify certain ACT scores while at the same time knowing that the difference between a twenty-three and a twenty-six on that test is nearly indistinguishable in real-life application. Many schools have opted to raise the ceiling for grade point averages beyond 4.0.

Why? Competition. Some classes, after all, are much more difficult and therefore much more valuable than others. Never mind that not a single one of us in education is capable of measuring intelligence, capabilities, or potential—that is not at all why we willingly play these little games.

We play the measuring game with our public because moms and dads want exactly what they wanted twelve years earlier when they met with preschool personnel. Now, however, it is not about Johnnie's abilities to play well with others, it is whether or not he will be appropriately recognized for his efforts in advanced placement courses. Besides, a 4.2 GPA sounds so much cooler than a plain-old, boring 4.0 GPA.

Somewhere along the line, the adults in the lives of our current students have forgotten that the measuring and comparing of abilities and talents is worthless if it does not improve those who are being measured and compared. Being competitive is a fantastic trait for almost anyone in any walk of life.

However, the adults teaching and raising our young people are not teaching the brand of competitiveness many of our parents taught us. That is, there is only one person any of us can control, self—and even that is sometimes iffy.

Success is not attained by driving a nicer car than the neighbor. Having a higher ACT score than most of the class is not success. Being a better volleyball player than anyone else on the team is not what makes one successful. Success, according to my mom and dad, was doing the best I could do and, interestingly enough, refusing to compare myself to others.

Ironically, the comparison and measurement games we adults are teaching our children are making our young people less successful. If the goal is merely to win more awards than the kid across the street, we had all better hope the kid across the street is incredibly gifted and talented.

. . . IN SPORTS

If competitiveness and the need to compare is this evident in the scholarly setting, where educators are lamenting the public's apathy toward high school academia, it should surprise no one in education that high school sports are suffering from a tidal wave of this craziness.

The need to win, coupled with the necessity to look good while doing it, has made success in high school sports difficult for many to attain. The ideal situation for many parents of high school athletes is as follows: The team wins, and their child plays a vital role in these victories. Anything short of this standard can and often does result in parental unrest.

Winning, of course, can keep things relatively quiet for high school coaches and administrators. The concerned, sport crazy public knows enough to avoid significant confrontations about the roles their sons or daughters are fulfilling while a team is winning most of its games. In one of life's most glaring cases of irony, crazy sport parents do not want to be perceived as either stupid or ignorant of what it takes for a team to be successful.

After all, in their eyes, calling the coach or meeting with the activities director about playing time for their child should result in a very brief lecture from the school official about winning and losing and how the situation is obviously well under control—because the team is winning at the moment. This, as great coaches already know, is what the crazies have adopted as sport truth.

So when a team is winning, and a crazy sport parent is still unhappy about their child's role, they utilize a different bag of tricks. This is when some people resort to tactics they themselves can hardly rationalize. Because a coach is good when he or she wins, according to crazy sport parent ideals, some parents come to school officials with other methods of obtaining the success they need.

During my first year as a dean of students, the varsity girls basketball team at my school was loaded with talent difficult to comprehend for a school with under 150 students per grade. It is not hyperbole to say that any of the top six girls on the team would have easily been the best player on 90 percent of the teams they opposed.

After graduating, five of the top six girls in the class moved on to play college basketball, and most believe the sixth girl could have played at the college level if she would have wanted it. As would be expected with talent like this in a small school setting, these girls won nearly every game they played—and most of these wins were by an extraordinary margin.

The coach, although far from a perfect educator, was free from parental concerns and/or complaints during the season. Few people could justify being crazy enough to pester a coach who was winning games and playing all of his senior players. However, our administrators sat with parent after parent after parent before, during, and especially after the girls basketball season.

Why? What could possibly be out of place on a team like this? Note: There were several missing ingredients with that team. They were not coached well, their behavior was at times unbecoming of our school, and there was a lot of mentoring left uncovered because winning was far too easy for these girls. None of these issues were what brought parents into our administrators' offices, however.

Parents came to us because their daughters were not getting enough credit for the team's success. One woman, a grandmother of a starting player on the team, made an appointment with me two months into the season to talk about something she deemed "very, very important." When a woman in her sixties tells me something is "very, very important," I worry.

I was preparing to hear of an unwanted pregnancy, an arrest for drug or alcohol possession, something awful and completely unforeseen. Instead, the woman wanted to vent about how her granddaughter was being slighted by her coaches, her teammates, and especially the media.

"Some of these other girls are on the radio being interviewed after every damn game!" I was looking for a secret backdoor to my office as the woman continued her craziness. "And you know what? Some of these girls are mean as hell, too!"

The half-hour session consisted of explanations of how some of the top scorers on the team would never have "their points" without her granddaughter's passing, how it is common knowledge that a few of these gals on the damn radio every night were drinking beer half of last summer, and how none of us seem to "get it."

When I asked the woman for details about the girls drinking alcohol, she immediately backed off and attempted to refocus the topic on her granddaughter. At the conclusion of our discussion, there was absolutely nothing I could do for this woman aside from assuring her that I appreciated her granddaughter as a student, a basketball player, and a leader within our school. If only I would have been the manager at the radio station. . .

As it is covered in the *Good Coach/Bad Coach* section of this chapter, losing games requires much less creativity from those who do not feel success. Crazy sport parents are incapable of understanding that their kids are not as athletic as the group of kids who just finished beating them soundly. According to these folks, their children consistently lose badly for one of a couple reasons:

1. The coach is an idiot and not preparing them properly.
2. The coach is a horrible communicator, and the kids do not know what to do because of that.
3. The coach is a demeaning jerk, and the kids have had their spirit broken.
4. The coach may be a nice person, but he or she is not "head coach" material.

When do these philosophies reach the offices of high school administrators? Every sports season. The same year the girls basketball team was winning nearly every game by thirty points, the boys team was struggling to win half of their games. The boys team, by contrast, had one player that year who could consistently shoot the ball fifteen feet from the basket, and they were collectively the slowest boys team I had ever seen. In reality, it was impressive that these boys won as many games as they did that year. This did not resonate with parents and community members who were displeased with losing too many games against rival schools.

The boys coach had taken a team to the state tournament just a few years prior to this challenging season, but this was long forgotten by many parents of the current crop of players. Unfortunately, the crazies often have the ability to find a willing audience.

During one boys game I was supervising, for example, a school board member approached me and started asking suggestive questions about the boys basketball program, the players, and the coach. It became very clear to me that this school board member had been having conversations with concerned parents about the perceived failures of the season.

Finally, this board member asked the question. "Do you think he's (the coach) the right guy for the job?" I was furious. After taking enough time to keep vulgarity in my head and not on the tip of my tongue, I answered. "As slow as these boys are, it's a miracle they've beaten anyone this year." I meant it, too. The boys coach was a much better coach, on and off the court, than the girls coach. Sometimes, however, good coaches lose a bunch of games.

PLAYING TIME

Neglected thus far in the discussion of success in high school sports is the most prolific issue facing its participants: playing time. Winning or losing, it is challenging for student athletes and those who care about them to be satisfied when the kid is not playing as much as he or she wants to play.

Certainly, there are people, both student athletes and parents, who understand the complexities involved with playing time. These people, however, are nearly forgotten by educators because they require no maintenance.

A retired Hall of Fame college basketball coach in Minnesota conducted a fun exercise with his players before every season. Each player was given a survey asking them what roles they perceived themselves fulfilling, what goals they hoped to attain over the course of the season, and how they view themselves compared to their teammates. One question on the survey asked for the amount of minutes each player expected to play per game.

What this coach did with the information was educational for his players. Each college basketball game has forty minutes. With five players on the floor at all times, there are 200 minutes of playing time available, per game, for the team. For all of his players to be on the floor as much as they expect, however, college basketball games would need to adapt to an eighty-five-minute game.

Another coach, a veteran of over thirty years at the high school level, has adopted an approach of his own when dealing with players and parents upset about playing time. When parents complain to him about their son's limited playing time (and this evidently happens quite often), this football coach offers the following solution. The concerned parents are assigned with determining which kid needs to sit so that their son can play more.

When this is determined, they are to contact that child's parents and schedule a meeting with the coach so that everyone, both student athletes and all parents, is in agreement about how and why one player is sitting more so that the other can play. No parents have ever followed through with the coach's criteria.

Playing time is where it all begins for the crazy sport parent. It is the first step in the campaign of comparisons that kids and adults (mostly adults) need to fulfill their version of success. Winning a state tournament? Fantastic. Beating the rival school? Great. Being better than the kid down the street? Essential.

SUCCESS IN A NUTSHELL

The crux of a successful high school sports experience, according to many parents and community members, boils down to a game of comparisons.

Does my kid play enough?
Does my kid play enough compared to certain other children?
Does our team win enough?
If we do win, does my kid play a vital role?
Is my kid being appropriately recognized for his or her sport accomplishments?
Is anyone else receiving these recognitions?

Great coaches, according to the crazies, are those who favorably view the parent's child compared to the children of other people. This, tied with winning many games, is the expected role of schools to ensure high school sport success. School personnel who work to appease these expectations are fighting a neverending battle because, at the high school level, making crazy sport parents happy is impossible.

THE CONSEQUENCES OF EMPTY SUCCESSES

What does it really matter if adolescents, their parents, and school officials cannot agree on a definition for realistic success in high school sports? Who cares if there are some crazies out there howling at the moon; can we not simply ignore them as best we can? This is exactly what the vast majority of school districts are doing about the nagging conflicts associated with high school sports.

The phones in the school's office keep ringing, and administrators keep picking them up. People are consistently dissatisfied with one thing or another about high school sports, and the only people being blamed for anything are coaches, principals, and sometimes superintendents. If, however, educators were truly the only people hurt by the crazies' quest for impossible success, this book would not be worth writing. After all, we will continue to be society's punching bag if we refuse to stand up for ourselves.

Those of us charged with administrating high school sports, however, are now called to stand up for the student athletes. Allowing those outside of education to dictate standards of athletic success has created a situation that has all of us (the parents, the public, the educators, the media, etc. . .) chasing state championships at the cost of what we in education claim to be our priorities.

Who pays the biggest price? The kids. While they give themselves to the whims of the competitive adults in their lives, they are being short-changed in the all the benefits high school sports can provide—not the least of which is a sense of reality.

We high school sport educators love to claim we are simply part of the process to produce well-rounded kids. We tell everyone we want our kids to be "three sport athletes" and members of the band and choir and student council. We say these things at our parent-sport meetings while the folks all nod their heads in agreement like zombies who have yet to smell the blood.

We speak like this on the radio during the coaches' morning show on Saturday mornings, and we are applauded for our wholesome approach to working with kids. Most of us probably believe our kids should be well rounded, in three sports, and in the fall musical with Troy Bolton. Most of us also know that the stuff coming out of our mouths is complete fiction, and it has been for quite some time.

When does a high school basketball player have time to be a three sport athlete? The typical basketball season is from the beginning of November to either the beginning or end of March, depending on tournament success. It is possible for a basketball player to participate in a spring sport after the winter sports season is finished; however, many simply cannot commit to track or tennis or golf or baseball because there is still basketball to be played.

Immediately after the season, nearly every school has a dad or two rounding up next year's varsity and playing games, usually in a tournament format, against other teams from other cities. The events are not sanctioned by the high schools, but every high school coach—and every kid playing basketball—knows about these events. The goal? Winning, of course. If our boys or girls can stay sharp by playing basketball all spring, they will be better by next November.

And then there is summer. If a high school kid wants to play basketball, he or she is going to attend the coach's camp for two weeks, morning practices for two months, and the traveling squad that plays in one or more summer leagues throughout the summer.

Baseball or golf that summer? Maybe; it depends on whether or not the kid is talented enough to easily make next year's team without worrying about the off-season. Family vacation? Only when it fits the sixteen year-old's calendar.

This example sport, basketball, is merely one of the many nearly year round athletic commitment possibilities high school athletes are expected to uphold. Football, hockey, volleyball, and soccer are among the many other sports that come as closely as possible to demanding full-time attention. The "three sport athlete" is becoming a mythical character in our schools. We say we want our students to experience and benefit from all that high school can provide, but we behave like the crazies we detest.

If a junior in high school wanted to play soccer in the fall, hockey in the winter, and baseball in the summer, he or she would likely disappoint all of his or her coaches by either failing to uphold an off-season schedule or, worse yet, missing part of an actual season to fulfill the off-season requirements of another sport. And what about the band or the choir? Or an academic club? How about some time away from coaches? These options have become nearly impossible in some schools.

This specialization in sports has been realized because the adults in the lives of high school athletes do not like the thought of other kids from other towns getting better at their sports while their kids stay the same. It is here that the irony of ironies exists about success in high school sports.

It is this very quest for success that causes the most disappointment for our student athletes and, subsequently, the adults who either care for or educate them. Here are a few realities about sport specialization:

1. High school athletes do not improve at a camps or while playing for traveling teams. At best, they will be given some ideas to improve themselves after the camp—when no one is watching. Most traveling teams have one or two players who touch the ball, or puck, while others are assigned to play defense and pass.

2. Traveling teams (outside of season) are a waste of time and money for most players. The vast majority of athletes are better served working on their skills alone or with a buddy at home. If a 6'6" kid needs to develop his skills with the ball, for example, spending his summer traveling to parts unknown to watch his 6'1" point guard buddy shoot all day is not going to help him.

3. Most good varsity coaches spend the first few weeks of every season stripping their players of the bad habits learned via their traveling teams. The truth is, the dads who are coaching these traveling teams usually think it is cute that the 6'1" point guard throws one handed, no-look bounce passes.

4. Sport specialization does not make a high school athlete better at that sport. In fact, it often creates the lull that makes them worse. With this, the student athletes begin to build up a resentment to the fact that, despite committing an immense amount of time (and money), they are no better compared to their peers or opposition than they were beforehand. These kids are often told their playing time requires this level of commitment, yet most informed coaches know better than to expect the results they are trying to sell.

5. Unless high school teams are allowed to recruit, winning cannot be the standard for success. Most high school sports programs, therefore, are better served by viewing all sports (along with band, choir, clubs, etc. . .) as equally important for student success. If we truly believe that good athletes are best served by learning to compete in a multitude of sports, then we are wronging these kids by asking them to be "three sport athletes" while at the same time not-so-subtly reminding them that one particular sport of choice is more important than the others.

Most educators know deep down that they are still not going to beat North High next year, despite the fact that their team attended three camps and traveled to five different states to play in the off-season. Why? Because North High has better athletes, and no camp in the world is going to change the athleticism of a high school athlete.

So why do we continue to follow through with the lunacy of doing what we know does not work? Maybe we do it because North High does it. Maybe the other coaches at our school show this level of dedication. Maybe we do it because we fear losing our coaching jobs if it looks like we are not trying hard enough to win. Whatever the reasons for what we are doing, we know enough to know a lie when we are living one.

I coached high school basketball and golf long enough to have experienced both the highs of winning with good teams and impressive athletes and the lows of being embarrassed by opponents who greatly outmatched us athletically. It dawned on me after about a decade of coaching that good athletes improve themselves in sports, and this happens for two reasons.

First, good athletes are far more likely to adapt and improve themselves in a given sport. Why? Because they are good athletes. Second, good athletes generally do not need adults to organize them for the purpose of playing sports in the off-season. My best athletes drove me crazy about opening the gym and getting them the best tee times, not the other way around.

And what about the not-so-great athletes I coached? These were some of my favorite kids in the school, and they were often some of the most talented young people I have ever taught. Athletically, however, they were nondescript. These kids were not likely to adapt and improve themselves in the sports of their choice.

Why not? Because they were not good athletes. With this, there was not often the zest for sports with these athletes that great athletes have. Many of these kids needed to be reminded time and time again about open gym and tee times. Moreover, regardless of how much I cared for these kids, I could not make them better basketball players and golfers.

These kids sit and listen to us rant and rave about the importance of dedicating themselves 110 percent to being a better player, and we seldom think ahead of ourselves enough to realize that their next coach is giving them the same message. These kids would need a thirty-six month year to accomplish "three sport athlete" according to our standards.

Then, after the kid has potentially sacrificed two or three other sports and several other interests in his or her life, he or she comes to realize the inevitable truth awaiting almost every high school athlete: you are not good enough to accomplish the goals you (or your coach) have set.

It is not bad at all to face that reality in life. In fact, one of the great purposes for high school sports is to put young people in a position to learn about setbacks and failures. This makes young people better in the long run of life. However, this is also why we have been trained to praise "well rounded kids" and "three sport athletes." We have forgotten that by asking our student athletes to put all their eggs in one basket, failure becomes true, empty failure.

Three sport athletes who are truly encouraged to sing in choir, play an instrument, and run for class office are far more likely to offset the beatdown given to them by North High with some successes in a different sport or activity. This is why we want our athletes to be well rounded. It is our job as educators to remind our student athletes and the public of these things.

EMBARRASSING OURSELVES

When a healthy perspective of high school sport success has been removed, everyone who participates begins to look bad. It does not bother me if a grown man or woman wants to look or act like a fool in public, as long as they are not dragging a child into their foolishness. This is what is happening today with too many high school sport participants. As educators, we cannot allow ourselves to play a role in teaching our students to behave like adults at their worst.

What is success? I supervised a hockey game a few years ago, and the arena was filled to a near capacity crowd. The new arena, a beautiful and very expensive structure, had recently been completed, and the home team was hosting a rival school from down the road a bit. My job as game supervisor was to watch our student body and be sure they were a positive reflection of both our high school and community.

The student body behaved marvelously that night, especially considering the tremendous level of emotion in the arena, the tightly contested hockey game, and the incredible number of people in attendance. As a dean of students, I was proud.

As a man, however, I was embarrassed. The behaviors I witnessed from grown men within my community was shameful. One man, a father of a hockey player, brushed by me in the arena. His eyes were glazed to the point that anyone old enough to spell the word "drunk" knew this man was drunk. He looked at me as we passed each other, and he blurted, "I've been waiting for this shit all day!"

Other grown-ups could be heard, in unison, bantering an official for either making or missing a call on the ice. During one of the intermissions between periods, I watched from afar as a police officer pulled aside two adult males and advised them on their words and actions. This high school hockey game was as big of an event as the community had hosted in years.

Somewhere between the restrooms and the concession stand there was glamorous trophy case topped by a sign, apparently symbolizing the need to keep established values alive within the new arena, that read "Protecting the Legacy." Indeed.

Chapter Five

Knowing What Needs to be Done

RITALIN AND ROSIE

It was my second year as a high school English teacher, and I had a fifth period class that no beginning teacher ever desires. They were sophomores in a class titled Grammar and Composition, clearly one of the all-time miserable subjects for fifteen and sixteen year-old adolescents. Aside from this fact, these students were especially aligned with the thinking that Grammar and Composition was the single most worthless venture that a school could ever create.

It seemed like every student in that fifth period class hated all things related to grammar, sentence structure, and anything else associated with writing properly. It was absolutely awful—and it was exactly what I needed at that time in my teaching career.

Although it seemed like all of the students detested class and knew how to push my buttons, there was one boy who was gifted in this area beyond all conceivable recognition. His genius for doing or saying the wrong thing at the wrong time could only be upstaged by his complete lack of self control.

This boy could not sit in his desk, and as though he was guided by a dark force, he was absolutely driven to say something inappropriate any time there was a moment for him to fill the void. He was the first student I thought I hated.

After tolerating a few weeks of this boy, I removed him from his classmates (my first smart move) and sought to conference with him one-on-one in the hallway (my second smart move). I wanted to kill him with my insults, but I was too distracted by his affect to say to him what I had in mind. Instead, I looked into his wild eyes.

He was literally too wound up to be afraid of me; his eyes were like those of a caged animal, streaming from one end of the hall to the other like he was watching a tennis match. I will never forget the brief conversation that followed finally getting my wits about me enough to ask him a simple question.

"Why won't you give me at least ONE DAY where you stop acting like the devil?"

"Because I can't."

No other words were needed. It was the first time the two of us were on the same page since Grammar and Composition class began. I asked him a question, and I was completely confident that the boy answered me honestly. I had no idea if all day, every day was like this for him, but I began to realize that at least during fifth period, this boy could not control himself. Further, I realized for the first time as a teacher that my people skills and determination were no match for whatever this young man was dishing out every day.

I was not going to fix this kid by myself. I cannot remember how many people I spoke with after school that day, and I cannot remember who eventually had an answer for me, but the boy who was driving me crazy every fifth period was eventually referred to a specialist and diagnosed with a very real and serious case of ADHD.

As it turned out, the boy was suffering badly in many of his classes—and especially struggling in the afternoon. He was the first student I ever knew first-hand who was prescribed Ritalin for behavior control.

Overnight miracles are for movies and stories that other people tell. This boy did not improve immediately, and I still wanted to ship him away during many of the following Grammar and Composition lessons. The magic, however, was apparent after our Christmas break. Once again, the boy was a student in one of my classes, a literature course. I dreaded seeing him.

What I found, however, was stunning. He was a completely different human being in the classroom setting. Even his eyes, which before were often frightening to behold, were changed to a softer, calmer, and happier look. He knew it, too. The boy and I spoke often about his behavior change, the medication, the challenges he faced, and anything else he wanted to talk about. It was an awesome transformation.

Knowing what needs to be done is not easy for a beginning teacher. It took me well over a year in the classroom to develop enough skill to recognize problems and potential solutions related to student behavior—and my abilities were obviously still nothing compared to those of great, experienced educators.

What scares me about this story is the amount of time I thought about myself (and how unfortunate I was to have such awful students) when I should have been thinking of answers. Most of the issues educators face today can be viewed like this. Those rotten kids, their rotten parents, cell phones have made everyone stupid, the list can go on and on. The problem is, even if the finger pointing is valid, it solves nothing. We are all either part of a problem that exists, or it should be none of our business.

As a dean of students, I often took advantage of my "kid skills" by getting to this point early in the process. The vast majority of my day as a dean involved working with faculty and students to keep the ship sailing smoothly. This meant having conversations (sometimes very one-sided) with people, yet talking to someone, especially an adolescent, about a problem is nothing more than gossip if the chat does not lead somewhere better than where it began. One such conversation happened with Rosie, a frequent visitor to my office for various confrontations with teachers and other students.

"You got kicked out of phy-ed again, Rosie? What's going on?"

"I can't be by Desiree. . .I'm gonna beat her ass!" (Rosie and I agreed to be straight shooters. . .)

"Why?"

"She keeps callin' me a bitch!"

"Well. . . Are you?"

Rosie was silent. The conversation could have gone very badly from that point, but we pushed forward. I explained to Rosie that the first step to solving the problems we have with other people is to fix ourselves before we look to fix others. I used myself as an example. If I wanted to be truly respected by the faculty within our high school, I offered, it would be wise of me to first be truly respectful of them. Further, would be really dumb of me to expect other people to treat me like a king when I treat them like lowly peasants.

No, Rosie did not become class president the next day. She understood what I was saying about owning part of the problem, however, and that was a vital step for her in dealing with Desiree and everyone else upsetting her. When I worked with students like Rosie, I asked myself one question: What does this student need? Rosie needed to begin to see herself for what she was—she needed to take some initial steps toward reality.

Whether it is realizing a student's issues are beyond one's expertise, or knowing exactly the right thing to say at the right time, experienced educators are in a position to do the right things for the right reasons. When it comes to the craziness associated with high school sports, educators are wise to face themselves the way Rosie was asked to reflect.

This chapter is about "knowing what needs to be done," and that is impossible without knowing ourselves—and knowing how and why others perceive us the way they do. Leaders in education must find the answers to four essential questions if high school sports are to be an exciting and worthwhile asset to a school district while at the same time remaining crazy-proof.

ONE: ARE WE DOING WHAT WE SAID WE WOULD DO?

As a boy growing up in my neighborhood, I was fortunate enough to have several friends near my age within walking distance. There was always a game going on somewhere, and, because we were boys, something was always being destroyed. Our football games always seemed to sacrifice at least one of Mr. and Mrs. Erlandson's young trees, our baseball games could break a window anywhere—but Mrs. Holden was especially vocal about this fact, and Mr. Price was clear with his displeasure regarding our trampling down his grass.

Absolutely no one in the neighborhood, furthermore, appreciated our bicycles rode or parked in their driveways or yards. We were a fantastic mess of boys.

We were warned about these issues nearly every time we played a sport or whatever else we did, and we knew exactly how serious the warnings were. Mrs. Erlandson? This was the nicest woman in the world. "Boys, please, please, please. . .don't play near those trees."

Translation: "Boys, in about twenty-five minutes I am going to bring out cookies for all of you (her son was one of us), and I am not going to do a thing about the fact that you will all treat these young trees like tackling dummies for the rest of the day. . ." The Erlandsons had the best yard for football because of the trees—they set up perfectly, at both ends of the yard, as the end zones. This, along with the nicest woman in the world as a host, was ideal.

Mr. Price? This was a much different story. To begin, Mr. Price was a pleasant man. He knew all of our names, who our parents were, what sports we liked, and he even took us all to the Dairy Queen once in a while. I remember thinking that he must have worked very hard at his job because he moved slowly and stiffly when he got home before supper. He almost always had a smile for us, however. None of us were afraid of Mr. Price, but every last one of us respected him.

Except for once, we did not play football or baseball or anything in the Prices' back yard—and they had the best "sport yard" in our neighborhood. When Mr. Price told his son (one of us) and us to stay off his yard with our bikes and our baseball bats, he meant it. He instructed us to play on the vacant lot next door, where there was actually more room. His yard was tempting, however, because it was so smooth and easy for running.

We found out how serious his warning was when he came home from work once to find us scrambling to look innocent. What we boys heard from Mr. Price at that point was enough to keep us on the vacant lot for good. None of us ever wanted to mess with Mr. Price again. We did, however, accept his willingness to buy us treats at the Dairy Queen.

Too many educational leaders are the Mrs. Erlandsons of high school sports. Nearly every parent-sport meeting, for example, involves a high school administrator or coach telling parents that issues like playing time cannot be discussed between coaches, athletic directors, and parents. Every sport season, however, has a parent somehow communicating with a coach or administrator about playing time.

Playing time issues are now only the tip of the iceberg for those concerned with high school sports. And, aside from pride, what would stop any parent from acting on their impulses to get what they want from the school? These people have seen enough to know that when it comes to high school sports, we educators do not always do what we say we are going to do.

Coaches and administrators preach teamwork, harmony, open and free communication, and positive attitudes to our student athletes and their parents until the words sound like the Nicene Creed coming from our mouths. We emphasize the need for our athletes to keep their cool when they are disappointed or stressed.

Do we showcase these philosophies when one of our athletes throws the ball out of bounds while leading a fast break? Do we keep our cool at halftime when we are down by fifteen points to a team we should be beating soundly? Are we screaming at our student body at assemblies to sit down and behave properly two days after lecturing them on how they all need to use their self control to communicate effectively?

Do we stop the angry father dead in his tracks when he approaches us about how stupid the softball coach is, or do we let this guy have an audience with us in the high school office? Massive mistakes, front page news events, are not often those which hurt high school sports programs.

Sure, everyone has heard of the coach who struck one of his players, or the administrator who was fired for embezzling money, but these people do not represent the overwhelming majority of educators. The consistent, subtle contradictions between what we say we are going to do and what we actually do are what is hurting most high school sports programs.

The ultimate test for high school administrators and coaches comes when an "influential" person within the community wants to be heard. This is often when all that has been built up to protect players, coaches, and even principals and activities directors can be stripped down by participating in a conversation we said we would not have.

Maybe this person is the president of one of the local banks, and he is "just curious" about why a coach is doing this or why one athlete is playing in front of another. Maybe she is a school board member, who has some concerns about a number of "things she has heard" lately about one of the teams.

The problems with this are numerous. To begin, high school administrators and coaches do not know beforehand if these influential people actually have something essential to share. These people are supposedly trustworthy folks. After all, it would be unreasonable to refuse to sit down with the president of the local bank—a man who has supported the school district a great deal over the years.

From here, the issues can multiply quickly. If we think that other, less influential parents or members of the community do not know we are willing to meet with "some" people about their concerns, then we are truly naive. So our high school office either becomes a waiting room for those unhappy about sports, or worse yet, our reputation as educators becomes tarnished because we kiss the back sides of certain people whenever they ask us for it.

Why do we make our sport commandments in the first place? We should be doing what we do for the well being of the student athletes, our coaching staff, the administrators, and the good of the school. If our priorities stay fixed on something as simple as this, we can accomplish the essential goal of being trustworthy—in short, people will know that we mean what we say.

This is not to say that administrators and coaches should either avoid having parent-sport meetings or maintaining a criteria for what boundaries cannot be crossed in high school sports. In fact, these have become necessary and they assist educators a great deal in the management of athletics. However, because it is the little things killing us with crazy sport parents, we educators need to simplify our approach with everyone associated with high school sports.

Instead of giving a list of commandments for our involved parents and community members, educational leaders need to be more like Mr. Price. There is no wisdom in giving people a wish list for behaviors they will only follow when they are filled with bliss. High school administrators and coaches need to determine exactly what situations they will not tolerate—and then it needs to be made clear to players, parents, grandparents, members of the media, and even themselves. This can be done with smiles on our faces as long as we are strong in our convictions.

So what happens when the concerned school board member or the bank president, after carefully laying the conversational groundwork, slips into that which administrators and coaches have decided they will not tolerate? The conversation ends. They can be thanked for their visit, they can be offered a cup of coffee—but the conversation ends.

This is how we as educators can keep our doors open yet not become the roadkill for those with crazy in their minds. Want to chat with the activities director? Great, let's make an appointment! The list of topics to be covered are seemingly endless. Our schools always need donations, we always appreciate good press, the concession stand could always use a little assistance, there are great opportunities to serve the community, and new ideas for any of these are always welcomed. The list of untouchables, on the other hand, is short and non-negotiable.

Are we doing what we said we would do? There are only two keys to remember for getting this one right. First, we had better be in the business of protecting our student athletes, faculty, and coaching staff by following through with the promises we make. Second, and perhaps even more importantly, we must not claim in the first place that we will do things we either cannot or will not do. Mr. Price said very little and promised even less than that, and not a single one of us were confused about what it was he was willing to accept from us.

TWO: ARE WE EMBARRASSED ABOUT ANYTHING?

I remember the first time I was embarrassed to be associated with high school sports. I was still rather new to coaching as an assistant basketball coach with three or four years of experience. Like most coaches, I attended more than just the events with which I was involved. Many coaches are mentored to believe that all sports and student athletes should be supported; I am and was no different.

Along with supporting kids, I attended events outside of my expertise to watch other coaches work. How do they motivate? How do they delegate? Do they manage the clock well? Are they prepared? I was fascinated with watching good coaches perform. Honestly, poor coaches were just as fun to watch.

The event that made me feel shame involved a football game. Nothing breaks in a new school year like high school football games. The kids are excited to be back in the mix of their peers, and the weather in the Fall is usually as close to perfect as it gets. High school football has a way of bringing a community together that few other events can accomplish.

A Friday night high school football game, in many communities, is the highlight of the week. One Friday night early in my educational career, however, made me question high school sports, and those of us who coach, in a way that has stayed with me ever since.

I arrived at the game late enough to miss the opening kickoff, and this meant I would have trouble finding a seat without walking through and over every living person in town—or so it seemed. I opted, therefore, to position myself alongside the superintendent of schools, the high school principal, and the activities director, who were standing on the track between the bleachers and the field. Their "spot" was absolutely ideal for watching the game, and I am quite sure I overstepped my bounds by adding myself to the administrative mix.

These three men were officially supervising the game, a job I would master years later in my career. Whatever reasoning I had to include myself within their ranks, I benefited from a great perspective of both the football game ahead of me and the mixture of our student body and community behind me.

The game was closely contested, and the emotions on the sideline were running hot. The head coach from our school was arguing with the officials and screaming at his players extensively—and, at times, with great disrespect. Although new to my profession, I was wise enough to say nothing to the administrators in my presence.

I paid attention to everything, however. How were his players reacting to these tirades toward the officials? Perhaps because it was expected behavior from their coach, the players impressively seemed oblivious to his rantings.

Everyone else paid great attention. I periodically positioned myself to see some of the parents seated up front in the bleachers. When the football coach exploded with something newly offensive, these people carried a blank expression, as people react to a sad scene involving a mentally ill person acting out in public. Sometimes there is nothing to say.

And the three administrators standing near me? Our conversation, which was cordial and lighthearted before things heated up on the field, became nonexistent. Absolutely nothing was said. My mind was working fast and furiously to put into perspective what I was witnessing from this high school football coach. This was a situation I truly wanted to understand. And then it happened.

One of the players from our school, a talented and essential member of the defense, was slow to get himself off the ground after a pile-up. I did not notice the coach walking towards him on the field as the boy hobbled to the sideline. I did, however, hear the coach as he came within about twenty feet of the player.

"Don't give me any of that fuckin' limping shit!"

I thought the whole world heard those words. As it turns out, the only people who heard the coach blurt this sentence were all of his players, the referees, the superintendent of schools, the high school principal, the activities director, a pocket of parents, students, and community members, and me. An assistant coach intervened, not to help the player get to the sideline, but to inform the coach that he needed to keep his mouth shut.

In probably the only moment of reflection he showed all evening, the coach was relatively quiet for the remainder of the game. It is impossible, however, to unring the bell when it comes to words and actions such as these.

Community members were angry and disgusted, and they should have been. The administrators and I were embarrassed, and we should have been. As I left the game that evening, I thought about the fact that none of us as educators did anything to stop the craziness we were watching in front of us. The superintendent of schools stood and watched as a coach belittled grown men and children alike, finishing with a profane dismissal of a student athlete that could be heard forty yards away. What are we about, I wondered, if we do nothing about messes like this? This is a question I am still asking.

Tales like this may or may not be common within high school sports as a whole. Certainly, anyone affiliated with education would shudder at the thought of coaches behaving like thugs for their players and the world to see. That acknowledged, it does not take a story like that of the vulgar football coach to make educators embarrassed about what is happening in high school sports; most school districts have their own little black eyes, those embarrassing realities we all wish would disappear.

Every school district has the uncle that no one (or everyone) wants to talk about. We need to think about the short list of issues that embarrass us and ask ourselves why we are not correcting them immediately. Is there a coach who consistently crosses the line? If so, does this person ever truly answer to anyone for his or her behaviors? I was not an administrator when the football coach described above behaved so badly, so I have no idea if he was ever confronted by his superiors for his disgusting words and actions.

I do know that on the following Friday evening, when the football team played their next game, he was on the sidelines coaching. I also know that he did not issue a public apology of any sort for his wrong-doings. Our school district failed both our community and ourselves by allowing this terrible behavior to exist without appropriately owning up to it. What are the consequences to a mistake like this?

Although the coach is no longer affiliated with this particular football team (his decision), many in the community still reference this event as an embarrassing and disgusting story associated with the high school football team. Anyone who thinks that this does not effect issues like fundraising, for example, is probably still wondering how and why Tiger Woods lost some of his sponsors.

Are some of our teams earning a bad reputation for poor sportsmanship? A team can win forty-five games in a row, send three of its players to a division one university, and break every record imaginable, and all of it will be forgotten in one night if a player makes a lewd gesture to fans, a coach humiliates an opponent by running up the score, or a visitor's locker room is left in shambles after a game.

High school coaches and administrators cannot recruit its talent and therefore may not be able to control what happens on the scoreboards, but we can always coach our young people to be respectful, decent competitors. Moreover, we must always expect great sportsmanship from ourselves as educators.

Do a few parents make everyone else uncomfortable at games? If so, why are they allowed to be comfortable enough in our presence to behave like this? High school administrators are cornered every day by disappointed parents for meetings they do not want to have regarding something about high school sports. If there are adults embarrassing our school with their words and actions at high school sporting events, high school administrators owe it to themselves, their coaches, the kids, and the public to meet these people with one simple message—either knock it off or get out.

Screaming at officials, berating the coaches, and huffing and puffing like a tired four-year-old is not acceptable behavior from an adult. If school officials want to be champions in the eyes of their communities, they will not sit back and watch this happen while others pay the price.

Improving high school sports cannot and will not happen until we are honest about what makes us blush. Crazy-proofing high school sports must begin in the schools. We have absolutely no chance of keeping sports as beneficial as they can be if we consistently allow the crazies to identify with our behaviors. The crazies, after all, should not be comfortable in our presence. This leads well to the next question. . .

THREE: DO WE KNOW WHAT THE BEST PEOPLE THINK?

Every boy should be lucky enough to admire his father. The first time I remember being proud to be my father's son was when I was twelve years-old. My baseball team was in a tournament in a nearby town; this was one of the first experiences any of my teammates and I (except for the hockey players) had with traveling for sports.

It was a forty-five-mile drive for a one-day tourney, and it felt like we were traveling to a different country. My dad packed the car with a cooler full of food and drink, and, like the other parents, followed the bus we players rode to the ballpark. I felt as important as I ever have as an athlete.

I played shortstop for the first game, and we won handily. The second game was played a few hours later, and it was the highlight of my athletic life to that point. I pitched, and my team eventually won the tightly contested game.

The next game was for the championship, and, equally as important, it was the first time any of us were going to play a baseball game at night, under the lights. For a bunch of rag-tag twelve-year-old kids from East Grand Forks, Minnesota, this was as good as it gets. Unbeknownst to us, however, our coaches were feeling stress.

These coaches, despite seeming old and wise to us kids, could not have been older than twenty-one or twenty-two. Their concerns, after winning the first two games of the tournament, involved the fact that not all of the kids on our team had played yet. They faced a decision. Do they risk losing by making certain that all the boys play? Or, do they play to win—and subsequently keep some of the boys on the bench? None of us kids knew our coaches were debating this issue, and I suspect none of us ever would have known about it except for the fact that our two coaches approached my father as he and I sat in the shade together eating a hotdog.

"Um. . .Mr. Tufte?" My dad rose to his feet and escorted the coaches away from me. The conversation was very brief, and I remember well the only words I actually heard out of my dad's mouth: "Everyone plays." Despite the fact that my life in sports has not often resembled a Disney movie, we went on to win the championship game under the lights. The whole day was a priceless experience for us boys. On the bus ride home, we raved about our successes, each of us recalling our awesome play and ultimate victory in the tournament. With this, absolutely everyone on that bus had a story to tell; all of the boys were given the chance to play.

What made me proud of my dad was not the fact that he suggested that all the boys play. In fact, being twelve and eager to win, I completely disagreed with his assessment of the situation. I wanted to win the tournament; furthermore, he hardly knew the boys for whom he advocated playing time. What made me proud was that my two coaches had up to fifteen fathers with whom to confer, and they chose my dad.

This was not by accident, either. This was common with my parents when wisdom was needed. It made me feel good as a kid knowing that my parents were often perceived as a couple of the "best people."

Educators must not apologize for believing that some adults are better than others. Children, of course, are forgiven for their carelessness. Some children, furthermore, consistently disappoint us with their behaviors. They speak when they should listen, they form conclusions when they should still be thinking, and they boast when they should back off. These children are the reasons educators have jobs. Many of these young people learn and mature into thoughtful, productive, and insightful adults.

And some of the children we teach already display more maturity than the adults our schools tolerate. Although this may make all of us proud of some of the best and brightest children in our communities, it should also warn us of the potential for stupidity and craziness from a great percentage of our adults.

Why does this matter? Who cares if there are crazies out there? The crazies are the people making noise. These are the people demanding a meeting at halftime of the first game of the season. These are the people calling school board members about playing time issues, and sometimes, unfortunately, they are our school board members.

Our best adults are patient, and they do not allow themselves to overreact to something like playing time. These adults likely have jobs that keep them too busy to dedicate forty hours a week doting on their passions for high school sports.

Many of our best adults will never insert themselves into the madness of high school sports because, quite frankly, it is beneath them. Knowing this, educational leaders need to seek them. And, if we do it right, and if we are willing to hear what they really think, they will tell us. It is important to remember, as proven time and time again with high school sports, that those who do most of the talking often have the least amount to say.

Suggestions for improvement are very easy to find. Unfortunately, so is Fool's Gold. There are immeasurable benefits to seeking our best people and finding out what they think. What do our best teachers think about the latest curriculum plan? If they were not consulted before the plan took effect, who was consulted? This mistake happens all the time in our schools.

There should be a week-long seminar for principals warning them about the dangers of faculty members who beg to leave the classroom for the opportunity to run a committee. The best teachers do not get too wrapped up in the latest curriculum mapping plans, state standards, or committees because they are likely too busy teaching effectively and thinking about what is best for the students in their classrooms.

What do our best coaches think about the sticky situation we have with one of our sports programs? As a dean of students, I noticed that some coaches never seemed to need anything from their administrators, while others seemingly required daily grooming. Great coaches are prepared, they are organized, they have great people-skills, and they knew what to do when something goes wrong.

These are the people school administrators need to utilize to build up their young, inexperienced, or struggling coaches. And, like many of the great teachers, these coaches are not likely to give unsolicited advice. Great coaches will often need to be sought; the folks who will not stop talking are generally the coaches with all the problems. If the insights of great coaches are wanted, and their advice is followed, these are the people who will improve high school sports.

What do our best parents suggest for dealing with our latest school-community conflict? If our best people in the community are not part of the process, we may not have the results we want from high school sports. It is important for educators to remember that spending significant time and energy appeasing only those who make us uncomfortable will undoubtedly result in us making a career out of such efforts. Some people, usually those with the greatest ability to make noise, will never be happy with our efforts. It is the others, our best people, with whom we should consult and ultimately please.

FOUR: ARE WE MAKING EXCUSES FOR OUR FAILURES, OR ARE WE FIXING THEM?

What is the difference between a great school administrator and all of the others? Great superintendents, principals, assistant principals, activities directors, and deans consistently show up for work every day with the goal of doing the right thing for the right reasons. It is impossible to make everyone happy all of the time, and great school officials know this. Sometimes forgotten, however, is that it is completely acceptable for some people to remain unhappy.

There are enough excuses for unhealthy high school sport programs. High school administrators and coaches can blame the craziness on losing, which often brings out the worst in people. We can blame the media, which may struggle telling the story as it should be told. Of course, we can blame the crazy-sport parents. Everything, after all, stems from their inability to appreciate high school sports for what they should be.

Can we blame the kids? Even the most challenging of our student athletes are by-products of the apple not falling too far away from the tree, but we can blame them nonetheless. The reality, however, is that if excuses equaled results, we in education would be producing a far better product than we are in academics and sports.

What has our public taught us? We educators are going to be blamed for anything and everything unhealthy in our schools—sports included. Instead of pouting about this, leaders in education need to see this reality as a great opportunity to set the standards necessary for improvement.

When dealing with the football coach who embarrassed himself and his school with his vulgar antics, what were the appropriate solutions—that is, what should have the administration done with this situation? There is perhaps no "set in stone" answer to this. Unfortunately, the school administrators did the one thing that was completely unacceptable in the eyes of the public. They did nothing.

Doing nothing about something so awful can endlessly damage a high school sports program. Allowing this behavior without taking action makes the school district look weak in the eyes of the community's best people. Allowing it gives the school a poor reputation within other communities. Allowing it not only frustrates the other coaches within the school district, but it also makes it nearly impossible to lead them in the future.

How so? Imagine the reaction of the volleyball coach the next time it is suggested by the administration that she improve something about her coaching. If we allow a coach to drop the f-bomb on one of his players, certainly we cannot dare suggest a minor improvement from another coach—can we?

Most importantly, however, if we allow this behavior we have completely neglected to give our student athletes the respect and decency they deserve. When we make excuses for our failures and our embarrassments, we give the crazies in our communities all the ammunition they will ever need.

Allow our football coach to berate officials and players? How can we possibly expect better behavior from the obnoxious dad who yells at referees every Friday night at our basketball games? Moreover, how can we possibly look at our athletes with a straight face when we tell them they need to compete with self-control? When we allow ourselves to be ugly, we lose our credibility as educators.

Fixing problems requires leadership. Almost every school district has a superintendent. Nearly every school has a principal. Most districts have activities directors. These are the men and women who are being paid to lead, to do something when something needs to be done. I did not fully understand this until I was hired as a dean of students. My first meeting with faculty was wonderfully revealing.

These teachers, many of whom were and are great educators, cautiously listened to me as I laid out my plans for hallway passes, detention policies, hats, cell phones, the works. Because I did not teach within this district, these faculty did not know anything about me as I stood before them in a leadership position.

The dean of students position was new to the district, and anyone capable of reading a newspaper or a computer screen could know what I was being paid to perform a job with no previous description. One woman, a counselor, finally verbalized what everyone in the meeting wanted to know.

"Just exactly what is it you are going to do here?"

I swear, she actually said these words out loud. The room was silent. I remembered thinking thoughts like those the teachers listening to me were thinking. I remembered being critical of "administrative BS," the type of language that sounds polished and careful and sterile to the point of being completely ridiculous.

The administrative BS was almost a punchline where I did my teaching. Lecturing the faculty on this, bragging about that, promising something else... I had heard from the mouths of high school administrators what these people were hearing from me. So, "just exactly what is it you are going to do here?" In probably the smartest move I have ever made as a professional, I smiled at her and answered.

"I plan to earn my money." The eyes in the room collectively opened with expressions of shock. High school administrators are not supposed to talk like this, yet this was exactly what everyone in the meeting was thinking about. The counselor and I exposed it for the truth it was, and she and I eventually worked together wonderfully for the good of kids in our school.

What do teachers and coaches want from their administrators? In short, school leaders need to earn their money. Yes, it is difficult to confront problems. Yes, it is difficult to change poor behavior or performances. And yes, it is difficult to keep the crazies from hurting the high school sports experience.

Too bad. School leaders have every tool needed to correct the problems associated with high school sports (and many other problems). Great teachers and coaches alike are begging for their leaders to act like leaders and get after some of these problems with gusto.

There are countless within the silent majority of our public, as well, who are waiting to jump on board with some really good, sane ideas and make high school sports better for their children. These people need educators to lead, however, because they do not fully understand the issues facing education and the realities of high school sports. Clearly, for high school sports to be healthy and productive, school district administrators need their voices to be heard above the noise of the ill-informed and negatively motivated.

IN A NUTSHELL

Knowing what needs to be done is a tricky issue. To begin, if doing the right thing was as easy as having an opinion, high school sports would be utterly flawless. Instead, finding the answers we in education need to solve our growing problems—like those associated with high school sports—requires a great combination of experience, reflection, and toughness.

- Are we doing what we said we would do?

- Are we correcting that which embarrasses us?
- Do we know what the best people think?
- Are we making excuses, or are we fixing the problems?

The first step to making substantial improvements with anything associated with education, including high school sports, is to adequately govern ourselves as educators. When we have ourselves together with little or nothing to hide, we are capable of leading on this issue and many others.

Chapter Six

Having Control, Assigning Roles, and Owning our Profession

SETTING THE TONE

Setting a positive tone always works better than reacting to the negative tones of others. Great educators have known this for as long as there have been classrooms full of children to manage and educate. We do not wait for our students to drive us to drink before we react; we get things established early—and that is just the way things are going to work in our classrooms.

My first year as a dean of students was filled with extraordinary challenges. There were serious changes needed for the school (serious enough to create the dean of students position), and some of them were simply a matter of the adults in the building making a decision about something and following through with it.

Boys were accustomed to wearing hats, bandanas, and other accessories both unbecoming of academia and posing as potentials for gang colors and symbols. That needed to change. Some of our students did not agree with the decision to label certain items as contraband, but it happened nonetheless.

Cell phones were seen and heard throughout the school at all times. This, too, needed to change. Even more students disagreed with this decision, one that limited their ability to communicate via technology around the clock, but it happened nonetheless. The teachers with whom I worked were encouraged to be the adults in the building, not as monstrous ogres looking to hurt and hinder the student body, but rather as the mature experts who need not apologize for knowing what is best for the process of education.

This is what educational leaders (teachers, coaches, and administrators) do in our classrooms, in the hallways, and at the lunch tables when we know we are right about something—we do the right things for the right reasons, and we sleep just fine at night.

So how does it happen that we in education allow a small pocket of people to overrun what we are trying to accomplish with high school sports? If we have covered our own bases (we are doing what we claim to be doing and have a reputation for fixing our own mistakes—chapter five), we owe it to ourselves and our public to protect these experiences from those with obsessive, hurtful approaches to high school sports participation.

We already try this with parent/school sports meetings emphasizing appropriate home-school relationships, high school league rules detailing eligibility requirements, minimal GPAs for sport participation, school attendance requirements, etc. . .Yet, most educators associated with high school sports believe efforts such as parent/school sport meetings are nothing more than window dressings.

We are still being attacked, subtly or not, by people "who just don't get it." Why? For the same reason some schools allow students to text message their pals during an English test or wear gang attire that, by definition, intimidates or offends other students—because we let them do it.

There are a few direct, common sense approaches needed for the well-being of our schools, our sports, and the students involved. The four guidelines covered in this chapter lay the groundwork for leaders in education to be the adults among the adults, something we in our profession have struggled with for far too long.

SCHOOL OFFICIALS MUST HIRE GREAT TEACHERS AND COACHES, DEMAND GREATNESS FROM THEM, AND DEFEND THEM ZEALOUSLY

What is it that truly kills the soul of a great teacher or coach? No, it is not a run of unruly students or a batch of undisciplined, uncoordinated athletes. Kids are kids, and finding ourselves in a position to deal with challenging students and athletes is as predictable as the next sunrise. No, it is not even crazy parents. Great teachers and coaches know the reality of the world of education, where even our best work will be scrutinized by the ill-informed and obsessively passionate.

Poor to average teachers and coaches may head to the hills to sell insurance when kids behave badly in class or parents spread their insanity throughout the school district, but great educators can overcome these challenges—provided their leaders defend them for their expertise. What kills the great teachers and coaches is the absence of protection from their administration when it is needed most.

As a dean, I sat through one meeting after another with students who were angry or disappointed with one of their teachers. It was paramount that the teachers within my school trusted me with these situations. Hearing a student say something like, "Mrs. Anderson is so mean all the time," required very little intelligence from me to interpret the message for what it really was— "Mrs. Anderson does not tolerate me acting like an idiot in class, and the reason I am in your office at this moment, Mr. Tufte, is because I acted like one."

The Mrs. Andersons of our schools need to know that her administrators do not get dragged into the muddy stories told by ninth grade boys and girls who are still learning how to be people. Kids are kids, and we realize they are ripe for misbehaving and should not be abused because of it. Yet administrators owe it to their teachers (and students) to remember that our students are kids—and our faculty and coaches are adults.

The issue becomes more serious, however, when a parent becomes dissatisfied with Mrs. Anderson. Why does my son get in trouble in her class every day while others do not? Why does she have favorite students? Why did she embarrass him in front of his classmates the other day? What are you going to do about this, Mr. Tufte? These are the moments that can make or break teaching careers.

Successful administrators understand that there is no such thing as a true, black and white story. Mrs. Anderson is not a perfect teacher, and she, like every teacher, makes dozens of mistakes every day. When a parent met with me to complain about a teacher or a coach, my first move was to wait, listen, and take mental notes.

Was there anything I did not already know?—seldom. Was there any part of the story the student has neglected to tell the parent?—almost always. Was logic and common sense being neglected in place of elevated emotions?— almost always.

When the parent finished with his or her concerns, I took my turn to speak. Usually, my best approach with folks was to fill in the missing pieces of the story: "No, Mrs. Anderson did not say that to your son in class, I said it to him in this office. And, actually, sir, I think your son neglected to tell you about. . ."

What if Mrs. Anderson is making mistakes with her students? Perhaps she does appear to treat some students more favorably than others, for example. This happens, and good administrators would work with her to improve these skills and habits. However, good administrators do not allow themselves to sacrifice Mrs. Anderson's good name and hard work by rewarding poor be-havior from a student and anger from this student's parents to cloud the big picture.

Unless something horrible or unavoidable shows itself, good administra-tors reprimand and coach their teachers privately; they praise and support them publicly. The payoff of this philosophy? Good teachers become great teachers, and they feel both trusted and empowered by their superiors.

Coaches of high school sports, however, often struggle to feel this trust and empowerment. Why? To begin, coaches of high school sports are scruti-nized by members of the community on a daily basis, yet they are very seldom coached by their administrators to be better coaches themselves. Instead, these coaches often continue with methods and approaches that could have easily improved with any appropriate mentoring.

Second, coaches are not defended and praised enough by their administra-tors when the moment requires such assistance. Ironically, coaches of high school sports need this assistance from administrators far more frequently than most teachers will ever need. Why? Because sports stir more passion than academics, and the race is not even close.

High school coaches are often not pushed by their bosses to be great because most school districts have no standard for coaching greatness aside from whatever the public dictates greatness to be. The problem with this truth is beyond obvious. Wins and losses, for example, can be viewed by many in a community as the determinant of a successful high school sports program – and coach. However, I have personally witnessed lousy coaches taking teams to state tournaments, while Hall of Fame coaches finish seasons nine games under .500. This is how we want to determine quality?

Administrators, especially activities directors, are sometimes stuck be-cause they feel like a foreigner to some sports. Many schools districts have soccer teams, for example, and the only adult employed by the district who knows anything significant about soccer is the head coach.

Soccer was not popular in our country twenty-five years ago when our current activities directors were playing high school sports. Soccer was for Europeans and kids who could not hit baseballs; now some of our best athletes play this great game.

Too often, the side effect of a situation like this is that the activities director and other administrators remove themselves nearly completely from the soccer program because the coach obviously knows more than anything an administrator could ever know. What is forgotten, however, is that soccer coaches are no different from our English, math, and science teachers. Knowledge of a subject material, such as soccer, is only a piece of the puzzle.

Just like teachers, coaches need skills with communicating, motivating, managing, organizing, dealing with success, dealing with failure, etc. . .So when coaches in situations like these begin to struggle with the "people skill" areas of their work, they are difficult to defend because they have not been mentored to develop these essential coaching qualities.

Even within the traditional and highly popular sports, high school administrators have been too casual about developing coaches to be great. Truly expecting greatness from teachers and coaches puts school districts in the driver's seat when it comes to battling the crazies. When school leaders are confident with the abilities of the men and women coaching the high school sports, there is absolutely no excuse for allowing them to be attacked by parents, members of the community, the media, or even school board members without aggressively coming to their defense.

The first ingredient to crazy-proofing high school sports is protecting coaches. If these coaches are skilled enough to be employed, they are certainly worth mentoring to greatness. If anything about that last sentence seems shaky to an administrator, either the coach in question is not skilled enough or the administrator is not strong enough.

If educational leaders are confident that our children are being coached by the best we can offer, then these coaches are to be defended. When school districts consistently fall short of this standard, their varsity teams end up being coached by men and women outside of education and often too young and/or inexperienced to truly comprehend the significance of their jobs.

SCHOOL OFFICIALS MUST INSIST THAT EVERYONE WITHIN THE HIGH SCHOOL SPORTS ARENA KNOW HIS OR HER ROLE — AND SCHOOL OFFICIALS MUST DECIDE THESE ROLES

It could be said that high school sports has too many cooks in the kitchen. There are the student athletes practicing and playing their games, the coaches organizing and maintaining their programs, the parents sacrificing their gas money and social lives, the administrators supervising, the school board members eves dropping, and the media folks broadcasting and talking about all of it.

The reality of things, however, is not that all of these people want to run high school sports. In fact, very few people would be willing to dedicate the time necessary to coach a high school varsity team for the twenty-five cents an hour coaches earn.

In reality, there are simply too many people trying to tell the cooks what to make for supper. It has become incredibly easy for community members to both keep a safe distance and complain about high school sports loudly enough to be heard. Unbelievably, sometimes these people even get what they want by taking this approach. This has happened because high school administrators and coaches have failed to define and establish roles for high school sports participants.

Instead of reminding the community that we are the cooks and this is our kitchen, we have made it a habit of trying to make everyone happy. This does not work. Further, why would we want to make some of the crazies happy? The ill-informed and the negatively active adult high school sport participants should be educated, not appeased.

Who is running the show with high school sports if it is not educators? This is not Europe, where there is often a significant disconnect between academics and athletics. In our country, the same people who oversee our school curriculum are members of the prom committee, and they are on the hook for high school sports as well. Many ill-informed scholars in our country praise the European model, mostly for removing sport from school.

This is incredibly short-sighted thinking, however, for countless reasons. Simply moving sports outside of school parameters would not eliminate problems. Rather, it would make them horribly worse for the people who matter the most—the kids.

If high school sports in this country have taught us anything, it is that the less of an educational presence we have, the worse off the experience is for everyone. Do we really want some of these "concerned" and passionate dads with all of their free time coaching high school kids twelve months a year? Those closely associated with both education and coaching kids know better than to make the Europeans role models for our educational and extracurricular needs.

This is also not AAU Basketball or Juniors Hockey or one of the seemingly countless U-16 All Star teams either, where one sport is prioritized over not only other sports and activities, but oftentimes academics as well. Unfortunately, high school coaches and administrators have associated themselves with programs like these in an attempt to provide opportunities in competitiveness that they feel "regular" high school sports cannot offer.

Whether this is true or if it should be available for high school student athletes is debatable, yet coaches and administrators have an obligation to these athletes and the parents to remind them of a reality that traveling all-star team coaches do not reveal up-front. In short, there are not that many all-stars out there. Want to be on our all-star basketball team, young man? Great, please tell your folks to get their checkbook out, and you really need to get ready to pass the ball a lot.

Those in charge of high school sports are responsible for more than sports. The high school sports system in the United States may not be perfect, but it is the most sensible approach there is for accomplishing what wise adults know to be beneficial for young people. Leaders in our school districts, therefore, need to be mindful of the importance of their roles as the guardians of high school sports. The first role school officials have to protect student athletes (and high school sports as a whole) is to determine the appropriate roles of all participants.

Who makes decisions about high school sports? What decisions are specific people allowed to make? Who hears the complaints? What complaints should some people be willing to hear—and not hear? Who is allowed access to our student athletes? These are a few of the questions educators face every day regarding high school sports.

If there is no consistency with the answers to these questions, the craziness will continue. In short, for the good of everyone involved, especially the student athletes, roles need to be clearly established by school officials.

Independent school districts have realities unique to their communities regarding roles for high school sport participants. There is obviously no "set in stone" method capable of meeting the needs of every high school, yet there are some essential guidelines all school districts must consider with the goal of crazy-proofing high school sports. To begin, the following people must know what is expected of them as high school sport facilitators and participants:

School board members
Superintendents
Principals
Activities directors
Coaches
Parents and relatives of student athletes
Students
Student athletes
Members of the community
Media

With the roles of these people established, conflict resolution can become something beyond an exercise in futility. Instead, these roles can lead to practical rules of engagement for high school sports-related complaints. This detail will be covered in chapter eight.

Who decides what role a parent should play in the process of high school sports? Educators obviously have no control over what a parent says or does outside of the school setting, but the needless stress educators feel that is associated with sports begins at school. This is where educators lead, plain and simple. Decisions should be made by experts. Superintendents, principals, and activities directors have been hired to be these experts.

TEACHERS, ADMINISTRATORS, AND COACHES MUST REFLECT THEIR EXPERTISE IN THE FIELD

The 10,000-hour rule has become a relatively well-known maxim in our society. In short, the notion is that 10,000 hours are required at something for one to be deemed as an expert in that endeavor. There are certainly some restrictions and exceptions to this rule, however.

A grown man who has played golf every day for twenty years at a 15 handicap is not an expert golfer, despite his wishes otherwise. Time alone does not make one an expert; many people can lose their hours in hobbies that provide them with joy and relaxation (harmonious passion) without the inclusion of mastery performances.

The 10,000-hour rule, therefore, must be applied with the assumption that the time used toward the activity, performance, or project is used with great purpose and with the goal of being excellent. Great coaches, for example, will remind that practice does not make perfect—perfect practice makes perfect.

Much can be learned about high school sports by applying the 10,000-hour concept. To begin, the chances are great that most coaches reading this book have never met a student athlete who has given that much time to anything associated with athletics. Professional tennis players and golfers, for example, are often reputed for their extraordinary dedication to these sports at an early age.

Tiger Woods was hitting golf shots in third grade that the best player I know has difficulty managing. With this, Tiger Woods was hitting these shots, properly and consistently and methodically, for hours upon hours every day.

This did not happen simply because Earl Woods was a highly involved "sport parent" either; if that was all it takes to make sports superstars, each year thousands of kids from Minnesota would be the next Wayne Gretzky. Talent and desire like this is as rare for someone that age as it is for a third grader to be six feet tall. Not only is it uncommon for high school athletes to have this much invested in a sport, it is appropriate that they do not.

Why? Because Tiger Woods is beyond one in a million. The kids we know, the student athletes that attend our schools and play on our teams, are not that good at sports. They play sports for different reasons than Tiger Woods played golf as a child. They become bored practicing hour after hour, day after day, because the sports are about excitement and relationships and reasonable competitiveness to these students—not attaining perfection.

Even the best athletes in a school district rarely find themselves paying the bills as professional athletes. Some do, of course, but these people are such an exception that for coaches to seek the recipe to produce pro-level athletes is an exercise in futility. Here is a reality worth remembering: Tiger Woods was Tiger Woods' youth coach. Educators, especially coaches, need to remember this, and they need to remember that the typical high school student athlete has not yet chosen that which will become his or her 10,000-hour calling.

But educators, whether they are teachers, coaches, or administrators, have chosen their life's calling. With 180 student contact days a year, a teacher needs nearly 7 years of experience in the classroom to amass 10,000 hours as an educator. Considering the fact that it may take a few years for a teacher or coach to actually develop an educational identity worthy of fine-tuning, it can be argued that becoming an expert in education takes a decade.

This is why the best principals were successful classroom teachers long before they became administrators. This is also why a twenty-five-year-old has no business, regardless of intellect or charm, being a superintendent of schools. 10,000 hours, if experienced with purposeful and harmonious intent, provide the resumé that a college degree with an impressive GPA and all the right answers in an interview cannot possibly match. Experience does not make everyone better at their chosen activities or profession, but inexperience can only be overcome with hours.

The relevance of the 10,000-hour rule and adults in high school sports is akin to this observation of principals and superintendents of schools. We educators expect our leaders to have both the honors and the battle scars to coincide with their demands. If our principal only taught for three years, or if he or she was of questionable talent as a teacher, this person had better impress his or her new faculty before insisting anything of them. If our superintendent was an ineffective teacher and a short-term principal, why would we expect greatness from him or her in this role?

Most varsity high school coaches have experience within the sport (or sports) they coach well beyond the level of expertise typical community members hold. More importantly, these coaches have likely dedicated years in the field of education, honing their skills of effectively communicating with adolescents, motivating them, setting expectations, knowing their limitations, and helping them understand that sports is merely one piece of life's big puzzle.

Most school district administrators, furthermore, have been immersed in education much longer than 10,000 hours. An activities director, often a former teacher and coach, has the opportunity to mentor his or her lesser experienced coaches similarly to the approach good principals work with beginning classroom teachers. Experienced coaches and administrators have put in the time necessary to know what needs to happen in high school sports.

If we allow the ill-informed to make decisions about educational issues, including high school sports, we will potentially hurt our students. Education is ripe for critiques and criticisms because everyone in our country, at least to some degree, has experience with it. Being a high school student twenty years ago does not make one an expert in education, however. Caring about the education of a child, furthermore, does not make one an expert in our profession either.

With this, watching football every Sunday afternoon in the fall, or even having played for North High in 1988, does not make one an expert in football. Caring about education and sports is great; being an expert is something altogether different.

For teachers, coaches, and administrators, perceiving and referring to ourselves as experts in education is not conceited banter, it is necessary. We owe this to our public. Honestly, what are we doing working as educators if we do not believe we know more about this profession than everyone else?

Most of us could not fathom walking into a dentist's office and telling him or her how stupid the decision is to fill the cavity on one of our back molars. We perhaps do not like the decision because of the inconvenience, the pain, and the expense, but most of us have opted to follow through with the twenty-first century U.S. protocol of maintaining healthy teeth and gums.

Why? Because dentists do not apologize for being right. They went to school for a long time to become experts at teeth, and we did not. With this, it does not matter to my dentist that I have had teeth for the majority of my life. He knows this, but he also knows that what I know about being a dentist and repairing teeth is the equivalent to what I know about being a surgeon after watching a few episodes of *Gray's Anatomy*.

Just as I need my dentist to be the expert he is, our public needs me to be the expert I am. It took me over a decade in education, well over 10,000 hours, to realize this. As a dean of students, finally, it dawned on me that most people do not understand enough about education—or sports—to make great decisions for everyone regarding these issues. I have learned, further, that we in education cannot be in our profession to make everyone happy right here, right now.

Ours is the job of building people to become better people, even if that means periodically disappointing them. As a boy, long before I earned my 10,000 hours as an educator, I was often reminded by my mother that 'what I think I know' and 'what I know' are two entirely different realities. "John, we can be friends when you're thirty. . .but right now I am your mother." She did not back away from being the expert in our home.

We also owe it to ourselves to be the experts in education. There is no white-collar profession with a current, collective lower self-esteem than that of teachers. We have been society's punching bag for decades, and our instincts for fighting back have somehow been suppressed, probably because it goes against the sense of calm decency we want our students to emulate.

We are a profession of servers; we spend long, hard hours doing difficult work that few people could do well for lower middle-class money. This approach, ironically, has made our jobs more difficult—especially in the area of high school sports.

Becoming an education professor meant moving my family. This, of course, requires packing up one house and unloading everything in another. During this process, we found ourselves well short on boxes. On a hunch, I tried Walmart at midnight. My plan seemed flawless. There were probably no more than three customers in the store at this time, and a truck had just delivered new merchandise to be unloaded and stocked.

There were boxes of all shapes and sizes everywhere throughout the nearly deserted Walmart, and to this day I cannot believe I was as excited as I was to see empty and available cardboard boxes. The problem was, the boxes were not available—not yet.

After seeing various boxes I needed for packing up the kitchen, I asked to speak to the store manager. My intention with this conversation was nothing more than to have her understand that I was not stealing merchandise; I would just be taking the boxes. Our conversation, however, put a wrinkle in my plans.

"You can't have these boxes until 1:00 AM."

"Seriously?" I tried my best to avoid sounding disrespectful and rude, but I questioned why I could not, at midnight, take some empty boxes home to continue a horrible night of packing up the kitchen. After all, what is the difference between midnight and 1:00 AM? Will there be a wave of folks flying through the doors at 1:00 AM wanting free boxes? I was tired, grumpy, and dirty, and I was absolutely not in the mood to go back home and return in one hour for what I needed in the moment. The manager appeared to understand my dilemma, but this did not change her policy.

"This is how things work here, sir." And that was it. The Walmart nightshift manager looked me straight in the eyes and without apology let me know, without feeling obligated to share the reasoning, that empty cardboard boxes do not leave her store before she wants them to leave. When I returned an hour later, she gave me anything and everything I needed related to boxes, and she did it with a smile on her face.

"This is how things work here, sir." What a fantastic answer. Chapter five of this book details the need for educators to govern themselves to the point of being in a position to lead. When this is accomplished, there is no excuse for us to behave like anything but experts in our field. We do not need to be jerks; that is not in anyone's best interest. We need to be experts.

When we behave like experts, we refuse to participate in crazy-talk with parents who have gone over the edge about high school sports. We do not allow ourselves to lose sleep about petty issues like playing time because we have much bigger concerns needing our attention. Experts do not need to justify every decision with a meeting involving mom and dad, a school board member, and an attorney.

High school sports are important. Ironically, they may be more important than crazy sport parents think. We in education know the difference, however, between what the crazies believe to be essential about sports and what we know to be. And when we disagree? Well, this is how things work here. . .

EDUCATORS MUST STOP BEING AFRAID

I was tired and grumpy when the night manager at Walmart refused my request for empty boxes. Within minutes of being turned around and sent back to my vehicle empty handed, I was also angry. How can this woman be so incredibly stupid? What is the difference between midnight and 1:00 AM when it comes to giving something away? How can she treat a customer like this? The rest of the story reveals everything I needed to know about the manager. Returning an hour later for the boxes was good for both the packing of my kitchen and a lesson about responsible, fearless leadership.

At 1:00 sharp I presented myself, tired and grumpy and still somewhat bothered, to the night manager. She was all smiles.

"Hey, you, we have some really strong boxes over here. . .These hold tons of paper, so they are big and thick. . ." She grabbed a shopping cart for each of us and whisked me around her store at about twice the speed I wanted to move. She asked me where I was moving, if I had sold my house yet, and if I had ever been in Walmart this late before. Although I was still tired, I could not possibly remain angry at this woman who was helping me with everything I asked for and beyond.

The two of us filled our shopping carts with broken down boxes. One of our last stops within the store was near another employee, who was busy stocking shelves. The boxes she had emptied earlier were neatly broken down and laying on the floor. The manager and this woman rummaged through these looking for a smaller box size, something good for "the kitchen drawer" every respectable home must have. After finding a few of this size, the manager and I started heading elsewhere, but not before the woman took time to speak two words to her manager. "Thank you," was all she spoke.

The manager explained to me that it had actually been common for people to come into the store on truck-nights and ask for boxes. Unfortunately, many of those requesting boxes were unwilling to wait for the night staff to get them emptied. This led to people literally emptying boxes of merchandise on the floor, leaving messes for the staff to clean up and shelve. The manager, I learned, was very new to her position.

When she began as a supervisor, she met with her staff and asked what it was they needed from her. Along with a few other concerns, the night staff at Walmart begged that they have more time available to them for stocking the shelves without customers at their heels. Quite obviously, this manager has found a way to honor that request, and her staff appeared to be appreciative.

Leaders in education can learn from this woman. Since I met her that evening, I have often asked myself who I am championing. Am I looking out for those like the midnight crew at Walmart, only asking to be respected enough to do their jobs without cleaning up the messes of the impatient? Or am I looking out for what I was showing myself to be that night, an insensitive and incredibly intolerant person? Educators have that choice every single day, and the handling of high school sports is as revealing as it gets for the quality of a high school administration.

If we desire to do the right things for the right reasons, we need to be willing to rest easily when some people become angry with us. Principals and activities directors would be wise to follow the night manager's approach as it pertains to leading a staff.

What is it that coaches truly need from us? How can we protect student athletes from the crazies? What are we not doing that we should be for our school and the people about whom we care? Do we want to hear "thank you" from our best people, or do we want to offend our best people while we try to appease the others? Note: The crazies will never be satisfied, so expecting "thank yous" from these people is futile.

Chapter one of this book, detailing the role of passion in high school sports, includes a story about five senior girls removed from their basketball team for various behaviors unbecoming of student athletes. The passion surrounding this event became terribly obsessive, and something as pure as high school basketball became as shady as a bar fight.

The local media jumped at the chance to show five high school girls, all recently cut from their basketball team, smiling for a photo in the very gymnasium in which they will no longer play. The entirety of the story is a perfect example of how a passion for something can become more of a detriment than a supplement.

The story about the basketball players, however, is also a great reminder about the necessity for strong leadership within high school sports. Anyone who has coached a team of adolescent boys or girls for more than a few years knows how easily a mole hill can become a mountain. When I first heard of the suspended senior girls, I was neither surprised nor bewildered.

Adolescents are volatile sometimes, and, if bad situations are not corrected, high school kids are not necessarily going to make the wisest decisions on their own. My immediate question was this: How in the world were things allowed to progress to this point?

Who was running the show with these girls and their parents? Situations like this one are the reasons we have parent-sport meetings and player-coach meetings before seasons begin. The troublesome behavior from these five girls did not come out of nowhere; that is not how things work with high school students. These girls and their parents had been pressing the right (or wrong) buttons for years, and they were never stopped at the door with the educational equivalent of, "This is how things work here."

Is it possible that a great coach could have made all five of these girls into fantastic basketball players? No. The root of the problem with these kids and their parents was that younger girls were outplaying these seniors in practice and subsequently taking their playing time. Great coaches cannot control talent level to that degree, but they can head off conflict before it becomes front-page news in the community. This storm had been brewing for years, and its resolution could have been found well before their senior season.

So why was it not resolved earlier? Fear. It is not easy to tell someone an ugly truth. This is especially evident in an environment like high school sports, where coaches have a tendency to tell a kid, "If you work really hard, develop your foot-speed, and become a much better shooter, you will be a player for us next year."

If truth serum were administered, the coach would be saying, "Even if you work really hard, develop your foot-speed, and become a much better shooter, there is a good chance you will not play next year." This last version is ironically much kinder to a student athlete in the long run, however.

And as for the parents, it is entirely possible that some of the parents of these five girls are incapable of feeling content about high school sports. What would have happened if the girls were told at the end of their junior season that playing time may not be available the next season? Yes, these parents probably would have been angry. Coaches know these realities, and because of it many speak like politicians to their players, the players' families, and the media.

Great coaches have a way of telling the truth and making it educational at the same time. People still get angry with great coaches, but they seldom have reason to attack. Why? Great coaches (and great administrators, as well) do their best to under-promise and over-deliver.

The five high school girls basketball players from chapter one should have known exactly where they stood on that team and what would happen if they made things unnecessarily difficult for their teammates or coaches once the season started. This, as it turns out, is as much coaching as having superior knowledge about the sport being played.

WHO, IF NOT US?

This chapter emphasizes the need for educators to take control of high school sports by assigning roles and assuming ownership of the entire process. In a society that cherishes sports beyond belief, high school athletics have become more than extracurricular activities—they are often the focal point of an entire school district. High school sports, therefore, cannot be treated with the same laissez faire approach many extra-curricular programs in school have earned.

Whether it is polite to say it or not, our communities do not care as much about the National Honor Society as they do the football or volleyball or hockey teams. Choir directors, student council advisers, and the prom committee, provided their work is thorough and timely, can afford to let their guard down now and then. Scores of parents are not calling high school administrators about how their child should be a tenor instead of a baritone.

High school sports, however, require strong leadership every day from a school district's teachers, coaches, and administrators. School district personnel are already held responsible for setbacks in sports, yet there has been a reluctant move on the part of leaders in education to thoroughly take the reigns of high school sports. This must change before the crazies take enough of the high school sports experience so that we never get it back. At this pace, it will not take long for that to happen.

If we in education do not lead the way for high school sports with our experience and our expertise, who will? We need not even ask this question; these people are already calling and meeting with us about their sports concerns every day.

Chapter Seven

Teaching Perspective

REALITY

As this sentence is written, my son is a seven-year-old enjoying a summer vacation. His typical day over the past few weeks has consisted of waking up when he is good and ready, putting on shorts and a t-shirt, and finding new and exciting things to do or explore. Except for one obligation, he has nothing organized or planned for any of his days. He is on a t-ball team, and he absolutely loves it.

My son and his teammates have been instructed to arrive at their field fifteen minutes before game-time to play catch and get loose. This usually consists of having competitions to determine who can throw a ball higher, faster, or farther. There are no practices, so every night there is baseball on the calendar (twice a week) there is a game to play.

This is fantastic in my son's eyes, for a couple nights a week he can put on his red uniform and wear his Benny "the jet" Rodriguez shoes (*The Sandlot* movie has been memorized). The kids play a five-inning game, and all the boys get an at-bat every inning. When the last player bats, regardless of the outcome, that half of the inning is completed.

The boys are told where to play in the field, and they are given a new position every inning. My son is having a difficult time remembering the difference between left field and right field—and shortstop just sounds like a stupid name for a position to him.

The other day, while my son's team was in the field, his friend was playing third base as both his folks and my wife and I were sitting in the grass twenty feet away. The boy started a conversation with his father while the other team was whistling baseballs by him left and right.

"Dad. . .can we go get a frozen Coke after the game?" Amidst laughter, the boy's father was trying his best to refocus his son on the t-ball happenings. He did not want his kid to take a ball off the noggin. Finally, the father agreed to the frozen Coke with the hope that it would have his son turn and face the batter again. Five minutes passed as a few of us inquired about where one shops for a good frozen Coke.

"Dad. . .can I have a large one?" It was glorious. This is what seven-year-old boys should be talking about while they are playing ball. The kid was not in the least bit trying to be cute, either. He was genuinely craving a frozen coke, and the smile he displayed when his dad caved to the request was worth the trip to t-ball that night. When it comes to sports with younger kids, it should not be difficult to have our sense of reality properly aligned; all we need to do is sit back, watch, and maybe laugh once in a while.

Unfortunately, not all adults seem capable of relaxing to this level—even at a t-ball game. A couple fathers of a few of my son's teammates fit this description all too well. Before the t-ball "season" began, parents and the boys were given a window of time to meet with their coach and the coordinator of our town's youth baseball program.

The purpose for this, in a nutshell, was to have the boys properly fitted with their uniform pants, shirts, and hats. One father used this preseason opportunity to speak to the coach, loudly enough for many of us to hear, about the ideal situations for his son. The following was covered:

1. The dad wondered if it was possible for the boys to have different team name. He made it clear that he was not a big fan of the Reds.
2. His son was best suited to play Shortstop.
3. His son will be switch hitting this season. He will hit twice a game from the right side, twice from the left, and the boy can choose whichever side he desires for his last at-bat.

This is no joke. At the games, this man made it a habit of sitting on his lawn chair next to his buddy, another father of a boy on the team, both looking like high school kids (these men are in their mid thirties) with their caps on backward and big plugs of tobacco in their mouths.

Early in the summer, the man with the switch hitting son was fond of instructing many of the boys where to go and what to do with the ball when it comes to them. He soon became more of a silent observer, however, after a few of the other parents subtly suggested to him that he was crossing the line.

Reality. When seven-year-old boys are playing t-ball, what should the adults in their lives expect from the process? Switch hitting? This act of craziness was pathetic to watch. The man's poor son struggled enough to hit from one side (not unlike every other kid), and asking him to try hitting from both was akin to asking him to use chopsticks with his feet.

His sense of reality is so incredibly blurred and distorted, I fear the future for his son. If a guy like this can be this crazy with a seven-year-old boy, what will happen if the kid actually accomplishes what dad most likely could not pull off, a career in high school sports?

This is what awaits high school coaches and administrators. There has been nothing done to calm the crazies in youth sports, and the next wave of ill-informed and unwise adults will be sitting in our gyms, our bleachers, and in our offices before we can blink. This chapter is about teaching the single most important lesson associated with sports: perspective.

If educators believe that theirs is simply a job of helping moms and dads teach life lessons to their children through the venue of sports, they are thirty years behind the times. These are the words we used with the society of yesteryear, the people who were too busy working to worry about their son's switch hitting ability before he became a second grader. Many of the current parents of high school student athletes in our communities need more than a helping hand teaching their kids; these parents often need to be shown the big picture themselves.

It is our job as teachers, coaches, and administrators—as mature adults— to teach our children how to view themselves, their passions, their ups, and their downs with a sense of perspective. Who else is going to teach this? At best, our students have fantastic parents who have rendered our jobs to be nothing more than academicians and extracurricular providers.

More often than we want, however, we are left teaching English, math, science, and how to appropriately handle losing six straight games in February while mom and dad are wondering why they spent a thousand dollars on camp last summer to make the kid win more. Educators, coaches especially, are charged with teaching perspective to student athletes. Rest assured, educators will be blamed when our community members notice its absence.

Reality is not easily found for parents when they are wrapped up with attempting to love and support their adolescent child while he or she is participating in something as passion-based as high school sports. Indeed, the mixture of love and passion can make even the tamest of people act like idiots. Our job as great educators, in many ways, is to protect these people and their children from themselves. We can do this because of a few benefits we have that parents do not:

1. Educational leaders have been immersed in high school sports for years, and most parents have not. Although we feel the passion, ours has developed to better understand the highs and lows of sport participation.
2. With educational leaders, love is not involved with high school sports. There is a level-headed approach to our work because we care about our student athletes without favoring any of them.

3. This is our job, and we understand the issues of reality and perspective in ways that parents do not.

So what needs to be said and done? If we educators are to be the experts with high school sports, how can we help our students and their families better understand the realities we know to be true? Our job as educators, whether we are teachers, coaches, principals, or superintendents, is to effectively communicate. There are perspectives our public needs to hear; it is our job to tell them. This remainder of this chapter offers some essentials all high school participants should be made to digest.

ESPN'S REALITY

It is impossible to determine how much influence professional and major college sports and athletes have on our high school student athletes and their parents. That admitted, there is absolutely no doubt about the fact that athletes on television have affected the mindset of both kids and their parents as they experience sports in America. Success, especially for many inner-city kids, has unfortunately been defined as being a phenomenally wealthy and famous athlete.

This has become a cruel irony in communities that badly need a healthier sports perspective. Nearly all of these kids viewing athletics as life's priority have a better chance of becoming lawyers, doctors, politicians, and teachers than professional athletes. Reading and writing abilities, after all, can be developed much easier than growing five inches, gaining seventy-five pounds of muscle, and becoming twice as fast as one currently moves.

Interviewed athletes via Sportscenter have become for high school kids (especially boys) and their fathers what soap operas are for eighty-year-old women. Is Brett Favre coming back again? Where will Lebron take his talents? Did my team pick up any free agents for "our" problems on the defensive line?

It never ends, and it gives sports-crazy people everything they need to feed their urges. But Brett Favre and Lebron James and Tiger Woods, when it is all said and done, are nothing more than tv characters for us, absolutely no different (to us, anyway) than the actors from *Days of our Lives*.

Two messages need to get from coaches and administrators to student athletes and their parents about professional athletes. The first has already been foreshadowed: These people do not exist. This is not to say that professional athletes are conjured out of thin air and presented on our televisions like characters in a Disney movie.

They are obviously real people, and they are obviously extremely good at their chosen endeavors. The reason, therefore, that these people do not exist is because they have become untouchables in our society, no different than Brad Pitt or Angelina Jolie. None of us, furthermore, will ever know any of these people.

So why do our kids and some of their parents need to be reminded that famous athletes are not "real people?" Because the second message is this: Famous athletes can afford to act like idiots, and the rest of us cannot. When Lebron James was given a platform via his own hour-long televised special to let the world know where he was going to play basketball, the job of every high school coach in the United States became more difficult. No one should ever believe he or she is that important.

There are high schools in our country holding pep-rallies and inviting the television networks to watch and cheer as young men, barely mature enough to get themselves to school three days in a row, choose the university where they will be playing football or basketball. The new, cool method of declaring their choice of school is to select one of the hats (there are various hats on a table, visible for the cameras, from the colleges and universities which have offered scholarships) and place it on his head.

If the kid is really a ham, he will tease the crowd by wavering back and forth a bit between two or three hats before finally selecting one. The present adults, most of whom are educators, at least appear to be impressed with the display.

High school student athletes need to be told that scenes like these are ridiculous. These kids are given their proverbial fifteen minutes of fame in front of their classmates, teachers, coaches, and family, and they have no idea they are being used by the ESPNs of the world. High school athletes need to know that we never hear from these superstars when and if they fall off the face of the sports-related Earth.

Did these young people have enough of an education to overcome their blown-out knee? Enough to maintain eligibility as a college student athlete? Enough to pay the bills when and if things do not turn out as wonderful as the moment they are living in front of television cameras as an eighteen year old?

Our student athletes must understand that if they behave at work the way they see their favorite athletes behave, they will be fired. Show up late for work like a diva wide receiver? Fired. Stop showing up for work altogether because one is not being paid what one believes he or she is worth? Fired. Belittle those with whom one has a disagreement? Fired—and maybe sued. Anyone who can behave like this and succeed does not live the life we live.

My own mother, afraid I would not understand the differences between high school and college, offered to me when I was leaving home, "No one is going to care how cool you used to be, John." Indeed. This is what love sounded like yesteryear. Our high school athletes need this message in stereo. We know better than to assume they will hear it from their parents, however. Educators must fulfill this "bringing you back to Earth" obligation more often than it was necessary in years past.

One of my first memories of disciplining an athlete during competition happened with a shooting guard a few minutes before halftime of a game against one of our rival opponents. Our team was playing very well, and the score was reflecting it. This player received a pass in the corner and drilled a three-pointer to increase the lead even more.

What happened after this, however, was quite bothersome. He turned his back to the court and faced the crowd of students and parents; he began to stylishly strut his way down the sidelines while holding his shooting hand in the air as if to scream, "Please, please, please look at me!" It was a disgusting display coming from an otherwise wonderful young man.

As soon as we took possession of the ball again, I called a timeout and removed him from the floor. At halftime, while his teammates waited in the locker room for their coaches, I stood with this player down the hall, and I wondered how I could speak my mind without losing composure. Finally, I uttered the following to him:

"I have never been good enough at anything in my life to act like that. Have you?" Fortunately, this boy was as embarrassed about his actions as I was. There was never an issue of behavior like this from him again.

Is there any wonder where kids learn to behave like this? Televised sports are completely inundated with these gestures. College and professional football players dance when they make a tackle after a twelve yard gain. Basketball players pose for the crowd and the cameras after doing something they could do in their sleep. College hockey players skate by the opponents' fan section and fancifully display their jerseys after a goal. Even soccer players have gotten in on the act. After a goal, players can be seen removing their shirts and running like a scalded cat to posture for the highlight reels.

And the ESPNs of the world show every last one of these personal celebrations. Before I am branded as Grandpa John, however, I will admit that I watch ESPN and sports on television as many of those I chastise. With this, my habits are as ironic as what I am willing to tolerate. We forgive stupidity from individuals if they make good plays and help our favorite teams win. Why? This is our soap opera; it is what "sports people" watch on television.

We have characters we like and those we do not. We enjoy watching college and professional sports, and most of us will not even try to deny it. However, responsible adults are capable of separating the athletes we watch on television from the athletes attending classes within our local high schools.

They are not playing the same game, they are not even closely related in their talent levels, and these student athletes will need a different perspective (and method of paying the bills) than the athletes on my television.

THE TWENTY-YEAR HIGH SCHOOL REUNION

Student athletes need to hear what happens at a twenty-year high school reunion. To begin, the whole experience is an absolute blast. Old friends are reunited, funny stories are told, pictures of everyone's kids are passed around, and men and women pushing forty years of age talk about their families, their homes, and their work.

With this, no one really cares who the best athletes were twenty years prior. Sure, there may be a reference to the class' best football player, the fastest runner on the track team, or an inquiry about whether or not 'that hockey player' played some in college. These are brief side-bar conversations, however, not anything worthy of a moist towelette to the forehead.

What everyone seems to truly remember are the relationships. People recall the nicest girl in the grade, the gal who would honestly give someone her last penny if that is what they needed. We remind ourselves of the boy who was voted 'most likely to succeed' and marvel at how accurate our predictions became. But no one at a twenty-year high school reunion is talking about or playing any competitive sports of any kind.

There are men and women who play some golf in the summers, and a few who bowl and try curling in the winters, and a bunch of people who pay the YMCA once a month and sometimes even use the facility, but these sports do not even enter the conversations. Why? Because sports are no longer a priority to people this age. The exception to this, unfortunately, can be found with the people already engrossed with the sports their children play.

What becomes of the best high school athletes? They become fathers and mothers, and they gain weight. The men lose their hair, and their wives are forced to tolerate it. They become teachers and doctors and lawyers and they sell pharmaceutical supplies.

Although some manage to maintain an athletic appearance, most former high school athletes end up looking like former members of the choir, band, student council, and debate team. That is, some look good, some look great, and some have struggled—just like everyone else. There is nothing magical about a high school athlete twenty years after graduation, at least not in plain sight.

So why do high school athletes and their parents need to hear this? Because the real benefits from high school sport participation are simultaneously powerful and invisible. Forty-year-old teachers, sales managers, and nurses have likely learned a great deal of the work ethic they possess from high school sports. Many, for example, first encountered their necessity to handle a bad day at work by coping with the adolescent equivalent via disappointment in sports.

And how do we recover from bad days? Do we pout about it? Do we blame others? Some adults do, of course, but many, especially those who have experienced what high school sports should teach student athletes, started learning as an adolescent (when these life-lessons need to be taught) in high school that highs and lows are common in life.

This also needs to be heard because high school sports need to be about appropriately handling our passions. High school student athletes are supposed to go a little nuts about their sports; that is what kids do with their passions.

Sports, if given room to teach, will give everyone an opportunity to deal with successes and failures and, eventually, an ending. In the end, when we graduate from high school and remove ourselves from the sports that have been so incredibly important to our lives, we grow enough to realize that there are other passions out there waiting for our energies.

Twenty years later, when everyone has grown into their adult responsibilities, it almost seems impossible to care about something like a sport as much as a kid cares. Further, twenty years after graduating from high school, if any capable and functioning adult has clutched to his or her past enough to still care about their own high school sport career, this person has not progressed enough in life.

So what educators and parents need to be drilling into the minds of passionate high school athletes is simple. Kids need to enjoy the experience and try as hard as they can to accomplish their goals and the goals of their team. They need to respect themselves, their teammates, their coaches, their opponents, the officials, and their parents. They also need to have fun, provided they understand that the world does not revolve around their interests.

One in fifty thousand high school student athletes will become a professional athlete. In contrast, the vast majority of high school graduates live long enough to choose whether or not to attend their twenty-year reunion. This fact is staggering yet so very helpful, if used properly, to educate our student athletes and their families.

High school sports are about educating young people to be better people both today and tomorrow. There is one catch that people tend to forget, and it is our job to remind them: Tomorrow almost never involves playing competitive sports with other people watching.

COLLEGE INTRAMURAL SPORTS

As a high school English teacher, basketball and golf coach, and dean of students, I have had conversations which have left me awestruck and dumbfounded. Adolescent kids will say the wildest things, and I think I have heard my share. A senior boy once told me he did not need to read his assigned English homework because he already had his life's work figured out, and it had "nothing to do with reading this dumb story."

I bit. What was his plan? He was going to be the guy who picks the "tunes" to be played during the cool parts of movies. He looked at me with a blank face and his palms up, as though to say, "tell me that's not the best idea you've heard in ten years!"

Before basketball practice a few years back, another senior boy (not on the basketball team) was shooting baskets in our gymnasium. This was a common event for this young man; he would shoot alongside our players, who were to be warming up, until we coaches were forced to ask him to step off the court.

His shots typically hit the backboard like grenades, exploding off with virtually no chance of going in the basket. He shot and shot and shot, and it was difficult to imagine that he could be any worse at it. Ironically, this boy was a good athlete, and he excelled in other sports. Basketball? He was miserably bad.

So there we all were again, waiting for this kid to leave the floor—and, again, he was going to make us tell him. One of the basketball coaches addressed him the same as he had been addressed on several other occasions. He was asked to leave the floor so we could practice. The boy, exasperated, turned and offered to my colleague:

"Coach! Basketball is my life!" If this would have come from a grown man, this bellowing would have been the most pathetic sentence I have ever heard. Instead, it came from a kid. This is the language kids use while adolescence has a choke-hold on them. Further, this is the logic and emotional maturity educators are dealing with every day—and the children are the easy part of our job.

Despite having thousands of head-scratching examples involving high school kids and the astounding things they say, I have never been leveled speechless with these children. They are kids; they are supposed to sound like idiots now and then. Our job is to gently talk them off the ledge so they can better themselves and laugh about these situations years later. When an adult steers into crazy-talk, however, educators often find themselves at a loss for words.

Most educators are tempted to conclude that moms and dads should know enough to avoid sounding like a child, but our reality consistently provides us with opportunities to educate the adults involved with high school sports.

A teacher and colleague of mine once took ten minutes of my life to explain why his two children, both in their early elementary years, were going to be hockey players despite his (the teacher's) career as a high school basketball player. He reasoned that because both he and his wife are white and short, there is very little chance his kids will have the genetic make-up to receive scholarship money to play college basketball. In his mind, however, hockey scholarships were a real possibility. This bit of wisdom did not come from a child, it came from a grown man—an educator, nonetheless.

College basketball? College hockey? The children of this man were still experiencing "morning milk break" and afternoon recess in elementary school when he offered this. If a high school teacher can think this way, it should not surprise educational leaders when those outside of our profession abandon all logic with their attraction to sports.

At its core, directing eight-year-old children into a sport for the purpose of obtaining a collegiate athletic scholarship is the equivalent of believing that reading and writing is irrelevant because one's future will consist of selecting the right music for all the cool movie scenes. The trouble is, whereas a high school student will hear from the mouths of teachers how flawed his thinking is, the crazy sport parent likely goes about his or her business with few, if any, people challenging the blatant idiocy.

Teachers and administrators alike would sing from their school's rooftops if parents concerned themselves this deeply about academic success at the college level. Whatever the situation of higher education in the future, there is little doubt that students would be better off with an aggressive, academically advanced approach to their education. If they eventually become college students—great. If not, very few people have ever lived to regret a thorough education.

It would be much more fun for all of us in education if, instead of dealing with the flood of crazy sport parents, we were forced to ask more parents to back off on excessive Shakespeare and Calculus for their middle school kid. At least when that brand of parent would go overboard, there would be an intellectual side-effect.

Somewhere along the line within the past few decades, the athletic scholarship has become akin to fad diets. Just as it is impossible to permanently alter one's body without a significant change in lifestyle, so too is it unrealistic to expect an athletic scholarship from a college or university simply because one is desired. Further, unlike losing weight, obtaining a scholarship to play a college sport is virtually impossible for many of the adolescents and parents planning and hoping for such a benefit.

In many cases, furthermore, the word "scholarship" is being used in households as dreamy goals for kids to aspire. There is no more plan for accomplishing the all-important athletic scholarship, however, than there is for people who talk about wanting to be a millionaire.

High school athletes and their families need to know that this mindset can be damaging to young people the longer it lingers. Seventeen year-old student athletes should not simultaneously believe they are headed for Duke University to play for Coach K while they are struggling to find playing time on their high school team.

When this happens, young people continue to view themselves as victims of others' decisions. Why am I not playing much this year? It must be the coach's fault. Why did I not obtain a scholarship? It must be the coach's fault. Why did I not get promoted as an adult? Well, it must be someone's fault. . .Reality is a fantastic by-product of high school sports, provided the adults involved, both parents and educators, are appropriately helping the student athlete deal with it.

Scholarships can be found, certainly, but there is a perspective to be learned that responsible adults had better start teaching. To begin, the vast majority of college scholarships for which high school students can reasonably obtain with work ethic have nothing to do with athletics.

Our young people need to be taught that realistic financial assistance for higher education is found at the dinner table starting immediately after supper and lasting until bedtime. It is called homework, and even if it does not result in thousands of dollars assisting a young person with tuition, it will likely play a role in college success.

An incredible percentage of college students play sports. Ironically, a great percentage of these students enjoy their college sports more than they did as high school students. Why? Because they are playing intramural sports, and the collars are off their necks. There are no coaches, there are no practices, and, unless one of the crazies has completely lost touch with reality, there are no parents involved with intramural sports. This is how most former high school athletes find themselves competing in college athletics, and it is exactly where these young people should be.

There is no need for rational adults, both parents and educators, to perpetuate the college athletic scholarship myth. It is not only acceptable to provide realism for our high school student athletes, it is a responsibility. Intramural sports are everything most college students need to fill the void left from their high school career.

The beauty behind telling our student athletes (and many of their parents) truth like this is that many of these young people will begin to enjoy the moment for what it is. Playing high school sports should not involve worrying about future athletics, it should be about taking as much out of the process as possible.

OWNING THE EXPERIENCE

The first chapter of this book discusses the role of passion in high school sports. Clearly, there is no lack of passion within the participants; in fact, it is the very reason so many issues related to sports have been pushed to the forefront in our schools. One of the worst mistakes many adults have made with high school sports, and youth sports in general, is that they have never truly given the passionate sporting experience to their children. Too many high school kids are not allowed to experience on their own the wonderful highs and lows associated with competition, sacrifice, work ethic, talent, and patience.

Certainly, it is healthy for adolescents to share their passions with others, especially closely associated adults. What a generation of adults have forgotten, however, is that the fire and energy and absurdity absolutely must begin with the child. From there, the kid can share it on their terms with mom, dad, coach, and friends. Adults, parents and educators alike, must reverse the trend of leasing athletics to the children in their lives. This method is, at best, not accomplishing all that high school sports participation can achieve.

Do we ever wash a rented car? Do we vacuum hotel rooms before we check-out? No, and although it may appear to us that our kids deeply care about their sports while we are equaling their passion, it is an illusion. We are providing them with the sport equivalent of a rented car, and our kids are not learning how to do anything with it but drive fast.

Adults are not necessarily ruining athletics for high school kids, but we are becoming increasingly detrimental to the process all athletes should experience. The most valuable of perspectives for everyone involved with kids and sports centers on the necessity that the kids must own the experience.

Robert, a professional golfer from northern Minnesota, loves to tell a story about his father. When Robert was a youngster, he was absolutely enamored with golf. With this, he showed great skill at the game at an early age. Anyone with a modicum of golf knowledge could see that this boy had talent that most could never display.

His father was a roofer in the summer months, and when Robert reached the age of work capability, there was a decision to be made. As the story is told, Robert's father gave an option. There was a ten-hour work day, five days a week, and once a boy was old enough, there was no excuse for sitting around and watching television during the summer.

Robert was given the option of making money with his father every day on the rooftops, or he could work at golf every day. Roofing was a ten hour job, and it put food on the table. If Robert did not want to work at that, he was going to work at something else. Why? Because it was not important to Robert's father what the work was, it was merely important that his son understand the value of sacrifice and dedication.

As can be predicted, Robert chose to work on golf. He played ten hours a day, every day, throughout his childhood. His passion for golf has remained throughout his life, as he is well into his fifties now and still thriving with the game he loves. In Robert's youth, playing his favorite sport was both a gift and a responsibility. Golf was for his own purposes, as his father had his own job to do every day. Further, the only directive from his father was that Robert learned to work hard at something he said he loves. After all, if something is not worth the sacrifice, it must not be that important.

Today's adults can learn from Robert's father. Having the perspective to not only allow, but also to expect our students, our children to own their athletic experiences is essential for a harmonious high school sport career. But what does this philosophy look like, and how will we know if we have accomplished it?

It begins not with how much we care, but how we care. Our adolescents need to sense from us that we love them but that we do not love the sports they play. Additionally, they must know that we do not need to care about their passions as much as they do. Moms and dads are not on the team; it is not necessary to attend every game to prove their love and devotion for their children.

Sometimes, like on a Tuesday in early December as a snowstorm is moving across the state, parents are well within their rights (and sanity) to choose an evening at home over taking a road trip to watch a hockey game. It is a good use of perspective to have one's son or daughter tell the story of a game now and then instead of having it told to them by their parents.

Adults can also teach the adolescents in their lives to own their passions by owning a few themselves. Somewhere along the line, parents have been conditioned to believe that they are wonderful people if they have made the hobbies of their children their own hobbies. This has been a terrible mistake from the start.

Adolescents do not need this from adults. Granted, because they are adolescents and therefore often find themselves to be more important than all others in the universe, they may want their hobbies to be everyone's interest. What they need, however, is the perspective that mom and dad and their favorite teacher are sometimes too busy doing what they like doing to watch them play a game.

High school students should also see the big picture of money as it relates to their sports interests. These passions are not free; shoes, clothing, transportation, concession stand suppers, and camps can add up to, literally, thousands of dollars a year spent on a high school athlete. The mistake most adults (middle class and up, anyway) make with this issue is that their children experience the benefits of spent money without truly experiencing the sacrifice of making any of it.

Today's adolescents need to understand that if their interests cost money above and beyond the family budget, they should be part of the plan to earn these funds. Teaching perspective about finances to high school athletes may boil down to having them understand that a three month summer job is what it takes to play for nine months during the school year. Owning something means paying for it, sometimes literally.

High school sports belong to children. Adults are needed for the process, yet theirs is a job that must not run alongside that of the athletes. Rather, adults are needed for the purpose of providing perspective to high school sports. One of the biggest lessons parents and educators can teach adolescents, furthermore, is that great passions must be cared for personally, not provided daily. Before adults can teach this, many must realize it themselves.

TOUGH LOVE

It can be conceded that parents of high school student athletes, crazy or not, love their children. Ironically, it is often this love that makes teaching perspective via athletics incredibly difficult for educators. Blinded by their loyalty and concern for their children, parents struggle to remember what made themselves transition from childhood to adulthood successfully. Many adults pridefully tell their stories about walking to school in the morning and back home at night, uphill both ways.

We recall the good ol' days of school when our teachers demanded both decency and hard work from us, and when being punished in the school setting was minor compared to what was awaiting us when we got home at night. Many of us adults are fond of referencing our old, grumpy high school coaches, who never sugar-coated anything while pushing their athletes to be better performers and people.

We remember these things, but many of us have failed to comprehend that these battle scars, these old-school hardships for which we are so proud, are exactly what children need today. Many of today's parents express love to their children by doing their best to shelter them from as much discomfort as possible. This places educational leaders, especially those associated with high school sports, in the difficult situation of trying to teach perspective to kids while simultaneously being perceived as the villains.

The new job of educators, therefore, is to help our community members understand that high school sports is still one of the best providers of life-lessons available in our country. Love, furthermore, is necessary, but not how many of us perceive it. We are not helping our adolescents if our love is in an attempt to shield them from athletic disappointments.

High school sports are exactly where young people should be failing. This is the greatest preparation for real life that many of kids will ever face. Failure and disappointment? It is inevitable in sports and life. Teaching perspective, moreover, is about helping our young people handle these difficult realities.

Educators and parents alike are fond of talking about 'giving our kids the best opportunities to succeed.' Although the intentions behind this expression are good, the words used hint at something vital we in education must correct. 'Giving' our kids the best opportunities is not what will make them successful. It can be argued that the father of Bill, the professional golfer, did not give his son an opportunity. Rather, Bill learned from his father what it takes to create opportunities.

Teaching perspective to high school student athletes (and many adults as well) is, perhaps, on as fine a line as that. Do we become upset when the child we love works hard yet does not receive playing time, or do we teach him or her that work ethic is its own benefit? Do we reinforce the often irrational highs and lows associated with winning and losing, or do we teach that the scoreboard is insignificant compared to competing against one's self?

Do we remind our young people that we adults have lives of our own and that we cannot be consumed by youth sports day in and day out? And what about failure; do we teach our adolescents to keep their athletic shortcomings in an appropriate perspective?

High school sports, further, cannot become more important than our faith, our families, our friendships, our education, our health, or our future. Responsible adults must teach both our young people and other adults that without perspective, our passions will almost always work against us.

These lessons are not easy to teach. High school student athletes need the tough love that many of today's adults received on a daily basis years ago. When a high school sport career is completed, the most important by-product of participation should be a further developed sense of perspective.

Chapter Eight

Reestablishing the "School" in High School Sports

CONFLICTING REALITIES

There is a significant, conflicting duality within high school sports. At one end, high school sports are capable of providing tremendous benefits for student athletes. It should not surprise anyone that, aside from either risk of injury or a rare exception to the rule, exercising creates an undeniable physical benefit. Additionally, adolescents who participate in high school sports have a potential for superior psychological health and better social skills than their nonactive peers.

With the likelihood of sports helping a student athlete maintain good physical health, along with the potential for these activities to reduce stress, increase positive mood, lift self-esteem, and improve academic performance, there are clearly enough reasons to celebrate high school sport participation.

School districts benefit from high school sports as well. Athletics are second-to-none at creating an interest in schools. A healthy high school sports program, in fact, may be the single most coveted trait of any school district within our country.

Our citizens do not spend Friday nights huddled together in bleachers to talk about the newly tenured tenth grade math teacher and her outstanding approaches to teaching geometry by using new technology. No, the folks in the bleachers are watching high school sports—and they deeply care about both the people involved and the outcome of the games.

School leaders know this, and emphasis is given within our districts to producing quality sports programs. It is no longer a secret that the easiest method for recruiting students to a district (and all public schools need students for funding), aside from a growing economy, is to possess a successful (winning) high school sports tradition. Right or wrong, sports matter to schools because sports matter to the people paying taxes.

It is ironic, therefore, that many of the same attributes making high school sports a benefit to adolescents, schools, and communities as a whole also play a role creating great stress and unrest for its participants. Where passion can serve high school sports beautifully by providing its participants with an avenue to either compete or watch competition, it can also cripple the participants with the weight of their own obsessiveness.

Passionate involvement in sports is further complicated for adolescents, their parents, and educators because no one can seem to agree on the purpose for everything. Why play sports? What should we get out of this? When pushed to reveal themselves, most people share their ideals for the purpose of high school sports. Unfortunately, it is difficult to find two people who agree.

So with a group of adolescents, their parents, and educators dealing with both immense passions and the reality that none of these people can seem to agree what high school sports should accomplish, there lives the problems associated with communication and relationships.

Success in high school sports is dependent upon its participants working and playing well together, often during stressful times. Stressful times, however, seldom bring out the best in communication and relationships.

And what about success? Much like agreeing on a purpose for high school sports, student athletes, parents, and educators are not speaking the same language as it pertains to success. Do we play to win at all costs? Is it about the relationships? Are we looking at the big picture, and, if so, do we agree on what that picture is? These differences are capable of making the high school sports experience unpleasant for its participants, especially the most important of them—the kids.

THE SCHOOL-SPORT MARRIAGE

In the meantime, educators have schools to run. Sports, extracurricular activities by definition, have grown in importance to dwarf many of the other responsibilities assigned to high school administrators. High school administrators, furthermore, have not been educated or professionally trained to navigate the mess that sports often create.

Principals and activities directors are educated and subsequently hired to provide a great education to students, and extras, like sports, are mistakenly perceived as fluffy, non-essential details in the minds of those in higher education providing administrative degrees.

What happens to administrators is often professionally tragic. They are painstakingly prepared for academic issues, state standards, and educational philosophies, and they ironically spend their days dealing with the crazies who care nothing about such issues.

Yes, sports matter to schools—to the point that many coaches and administrators have completely lost the grasp needed to keep sports educational. The first chapter of this book details the passion associated with high school sports. Obsessive passion does not coincide with the process of purposeful education. The classroom has become a nuisance to tolerate for many student athletes, parents, and, unfortunately, some coaches. For many, sports have become the reason for school.

What is the result of sports becoming something larger than the school itself? Conflict. For years great educators have been playing by one set of rules, working to provide an excellent education for the children within our communities. While this happens, many within the communities have been playing by a completely different set of rules, fully taking advantage of the educational expertise of others while they focus their energies intently upon the "extras" schools can provide—namely sports.

When this happens, leaders in education are consistently placed in no-win situations. Superintendents and principals cannot afford to spend 90 percent of their time dedicated to high school sports; there are countless other issues in schools demanding their attention. This results in situations like that of the five suspended basketball players described in chapter one. Basketball became such an obsessively passionate priority for these girls and their parents that everything else relating to school seemingly became a nuisance to them.

What were the grade point averages of these five girls? Were all of them reading up to grade level? Were these five seniors academically prepared for life beyond high school? None of the people reaching a fever pitch about these girls and their unfortunate situation with basketball were expected to think about these issues. Ideally, everyone invested in that story, including the girls themselves, should have been presented with these questions.

The school district, furthermore, should have required a policy to confront extracurricular concerns only after the priorities of academics are met with satisfaction. When high school sports overtake our schools to the point where these academic concerns are not pursued, both our young people and our schools suffer.

Leaders in education have long known that one of the best things working for academics in their schools is the presence of sports. Athletics, through necessity alone, have served to keep students in attendance and at least minimally proficient in the classrooms. Sports have been used as the ultimate big brother or sister for decades, and it has often worked marvelously.

What educators have often failed to realize, however, is that the tables can be turned with academics and sports to further meet the needs of both students and the schools. That is, one of the best things that should be working for the management of high school sports, especially as conflicts are concerned, are academics.

There may be nothing a school can do to prevent some children and parents from believing that sports are more important than school. However, when adolescents, moms, and dads are allowed to behave in such a manner, the school is just as much to blame for the consequences as the crazies causing all the problems.

Educators cannot afford to disconnect high school sports from the proper educational foundation, the anchor, the school. The very first move a high school can make to prevent ugly situations like having five of its senior girls smiling and posing for a photo in the gymnasium after being cut from the team is to have a rock-solid, non-negotiable "academics first" policy in place.

Why does all this stuff about sports matter? Why should we care about the well being of high school sports and those associated? It would be easy for educators to shrug off the issues hindering schools (and people) because of misguided passions relative to sports.

The truth is, if the problems addressed in this book were only associated with a small percentage of students within a typical school, educators could easily turn their backs and blame "those people" for their own failures. But we all know better; the typical high school has over half of its students participating in high school sports.

With that, educational leaders also know that these students care more about basketball, hockey, football, volleyball, and track more than they care about English, mathematics, social studies, and foreign languages. We also know that this is actually acceptable at this point in their lives. These sports assist us as educators because we can use sports to help us accomplish great feats with our students both in and out of the classrooms:

We can teach kids how to succeed—and fail.
We can teach kids the importance of sacrifice; we cannot enjoy our hobbies unless we work first!
We can teach kids how to work with people to accomplish goals.
We can teach kids that the best way to attain a good result is to focus on the process.
We can teach kids that, in the end, the world is bigger than they thought it was. . .

This is what can be accomplished when sports and school are together. Responsible, wise adults can see the beauty of both the youthful passion of student athletes and the necessity to mold it. Not everyone thinks this way, however. Not everyone understands education; many people are stuck in the here and now, the immediacy of the competition they paid five dollars to watch.

If it is possible, we can educate these people to think beyond their current state. If that is not possible, we must be sure that short-sighted adults do not become leaders and that their voices are not guiding our educational policies. We are the educational experts; we need to behave like it.

GUIDELINES

For high school sports to remain a beneficial supplement within our schools, helping students develop their abilities and maturity and giving adults an opportunity to share the passion of sports with their children, school districts must take control of the process.

The first step in this direction, as suggested earlier in this chapter, is to establish an "academics first" guideline. This requirement should obviously meet the specific needs of the school district, yet the principle of the guideline must emphasize to participants the reality that extracurricular activities, especially sports, are secondary to academics.

The format below is a sample used during my presentations for school administrators and coaches. I recommend every school district tailor a form like this to fit the needs of its educators, students, and community members (John E. Tufte School District has its own issues).

"ACADEMIC FIRST" GUIDELINES

John E. Tufte School District is serious about creating and maintaining healthy academic and extracurricular environments for its students. While extra curricular activities play an important, sometimes essential role in the education of our children, we believe our passion for these activities must coincide harmoniously with the academic opportunities and obligations within our school district. John E. Tufte School District is striving for healthy relationships and communication practices with students and families, and we are committed to our priority of "academics first." With these ideals in mind, the following guidelines will be followed concerning conflicts with extra curricular activities:

1. Regarding extracurricular conflicts, parents and guardians must have knowledge of the involved student's academic schedule, the teachers of these classes, and the current grade for each of the involved student's courses.

2. For an extracurricular conflict to be discussed, the involved student must have no current grade lower than a C.

3. If the involved student in an extracurricular conflict has a current grade lower than a C, a plan of action will be offered to improve the academic performance of the student. Extracurricular concerns will not become a priority until academic performance is satisfactory.

There are several details worth noting on the sample "academics first" guidelines sheet. Although some high school administrators and many parents of student athletes may initially believe it is petty to require parents and guardians to have knowledge of their child's academic schedule, the teachers of these classes, and the current grade for each course, requiring such a commitment is exactly what is needed to relay two important messages.

First, as important as sports can be, they will not be made to equal our academic pursuits. Second, unless something horrific has happened, our school administrators must not spend their days settling the extracurricular concerns of a student and his or her family when and if there are other, far more important issues associated with the education of that student.

Regarding the expectation of maintaining a minimal grade for extracurricular concerns to be addressed, this issue can and should be as unique as the needs of a school and its people. It is possible, after all, that a C minus is a fantastic grade for a certain student within a particular class. That admitted, it would be unwise to throw the baby out with the bath water.

Perhaps the solution would be to form a contract with student athletes and their parents when they first enter the high school sports arena. What grades are acceptable/unacceptable for your family? What course of action should be taken by your family and John E. Tufte High School when your son's or daughter's grades are below your standards?

Whatever is decided, it is absolutely essential that everyone involved with high school sports, student athletes, parents, and educators, understand that schools are not in the business of providing sports-happiness above all else. Academic success matters, and if the John E. Tufte School District administrators believe it is being compromised by an obsessive passion for athletics, sport concerns will not be discussed in its place.

The final academics first guideline is something good schools are already doing with its students and families. An effective "academics first" policy for high school sports should not be approached or delivered by educators punitively.

If conflicts exist between families and schools related to high school sports, there are obviously people who care about the adolescent enough to complain. Effective coaches and administrators can use this level of concern to help the student. It is not difficult to imagine a skilled educator taking control of a conversation headed the wrong direction.

"I know there are some things you are upset about, Mr. Jones, and I think we can eventually address some of your concerns with the soccer team... But I also think we have bigger fish to fry right now... Your daughter is clearly struggling in a few of her classes, and we both know she is capable of better grades than she is posting. I think we need to make a plan to get her back on track, don't you? I mean, don't you think some of her unhappiness with soccer is related to these struggles with her grades?"

Academics need to come first, not because we are mad or because we are tired of hearing complaints about our high school sports programs, but because it is the right thing to do for our students. If it helps relieve some of the craziness in the process, great. It may also make a few people wiser than they were before focusing on academics was expected of them to this degree.

The second guideline needed for crazy-proofing high school sports involves a set rules of engagement for parents or guardians conflicted with the issue. School coaches and administrators become the victims of the complaints of others, especially when sports are the concern. What damages many school districts is the completely open-ended possibilities it provides (or tolerates) for its public to speak about whatever, whenever, and to whomever they desire.

Like the "Academics First" Guideline, the format on the following pages is a sample I share with coaches and administrators during presentations on this topic. The Rules of Engagement Guidelines, as stated, assist coaches and educational leaders by protecting them from the ever-growing and all-too-common inappropriate meetings regarding their jobs.

RULES OF ENGAGEMENT GUIDELINES

John E. Tufte School District is serious about creating and maintaining healthy academic and extracurricular environments for its students. While extracurricular activities play an important, sometimes essential role in the education of our children, we believe our passion for these activities must coincide harmoniously with the academic opportunities and obligations within our school district. John E. Tufte School District is striving for healthy relationships and communication practices between and among school officials, students, and families with the goal of both keeping academics a priority in our school district and ensuring that everyone is treated fairly an equally with their concerns. With these ideals in mind, the following guidelines will be followed concerning extracurricular related conflict resolution:

1. Communication regarding extracurricular conflicts will initiate with the student and the activity supervisor/coach.

2. If conflicts continue, the student, the activity supervisor/coach, the school district activities director, and the parent/guardian can meet to discuss the issue.
3. All meetings regarding extracurricular conflict will include both the involved student and the activity supervisor/coach. This includes conflicts discussed over email or the telephone.
4. Extra-curricular conflicts involving parents or guardians will not be discussed until and unless our "academics first" guidelines have been met.
5. Playing time issues can only involve the student and his or her activity supervisor/coach.
6. Vulgarity, rude behavior, and/or threats will terminate all meetings.
7. School officials will not guarantee a resolution for all extracurricular concerns, nor will every issue be given a meeting for discussion.

The rules of engagement guidelines, as much as anything else, serve as a guard dog to protect educators from the crazies. These guidelines are only effective, however, if all the significant members within the school district (those involved with sports) follow through with the necessary policies.

It should go without saying that if the high school principal, activities director, or superintendent of schools simultaneously support these guidelines yet allow themselves to participate in private conversations with conflict-driven parents and other members of the community about issues like coaches and playing time, the process will fail.

These guidelines are also a fantastic educational, life-skill rubric for our students. In our business of education, one of the habits we must strive to develop within our adolescents is the ability to speak on behalf of their own needs and concerns. When we hold strong in our convictions about how we handle our sport concerns, we give kids priceless lessons about reality.

Is Suzie not getting enough playing time? How do we know this if Suzie's parents are allowed to communicate this on her behalf? No, if Suzie truly believes she is not playing as much as she should, Suzie needs to lead the conversation. Reality happens for this high school student athlete when she is faced with the following question: Am I really being unfairly shorted in playing time, or do I simply wish I was a better player?

This opportunity to face the facts is made difficult when adults, parents and educators alike, are willing to let Suzie play the role of high school sport victim, needing representation to right the wrongs she has endured. Suzie can and should learn from high school sports that any non-threatening issue she is unwilling to confront herself may not be serious enough to need a resolution.

In reality, the rules of engagement guidelines, if used consistently, will expose some truths about issues like playing time that have nothing to do with Suzies of our schools. Oftentimes our student athletes are not the people upset about the setbacks associated with high school sports. Many of these young people have realized their situation and made peace with it long before their parents make their voices heard.

When school officials insist that all parties involved (student athletes, parents, coaches, administrators) are at the table for high school sports issues, many of the issues educators currently face will subside. This will happen because most high school student athletes are more realistic than their parents about their talents compared to peers. Truth about a situation has a much better chance of finding daylight if everyone within the conflict is allowed to speak.

Kids know this. They know what they were told three weeks ago in practice, they know their current situation was explained at the end of last season and at the beginning of this one, and they also know that they have failed to share any of this with their parents. Lastly, they know they do not want these realities to be exposed in a meeting where everyone is allowed in the room and no one is granted anonymity.

This is why a meeting involving parents and school officials about non-threatening issues related to sports conflict should only happen after the high school student has spoken for himself/herself. Of course the parents within our communities should feel welcome in our schools, but educators owe it to themselves and their students to eliminate the all-too-safe, anonymous conversations that lead to coaches hanging up their whistles more than any other issue in high school sports.

When a parent is given the opportunity to discuss a non-threatening sport issue, a few essential pieces must be in place beforehand. As detailed above, the second and third rules of engagement have the parent involved only when both the student athlete and the coach/supervisor are involved as well.

Furthermore, as the fourth rule outlines, no sport conflict will be discussed until and unless the school district's "academics first" guidelines have been met. Rule five, regarding playing time, is absolutely essential for educators. Playing time must never be discussed without the student and the coach/supervisor present.

Vulgarity, rude behavior, and/or threats must terminate all meetings within our school districts. This message of discipline must be sent consistently; allowing ourselves to be targets of abusive language (or worse) will hinder us long after the meeting is forgotten. Students, furthermore, must never learn (at least from us) that poor behavior accomplishes the goal.

The best school administrators, regardless of their age or gender, will rise from the table, papers in hand, and announce the conclusion of the discussion once respectful behavior has been lost. Care enough to talk about your daughter and the volleyball coaching staff? Great, we can reschedule when you are capable and willing to communicate respectfully.

Educators obviously must apply this communication standard for themselves as well. Vulgarity and rude behavior from a community member can and will be forgiven. The crazy sport parent is either aligned with others who somehow support their scathing behavior as evidence of great passion, or they are dismissed by others as the "crazies" who make all the noise. Either way, poor behavior seldom hurts those who utilize it to meet their needs—at least in the educational setting.

But when a high school coach, principal, or activities director loses control, it is never forgotten. We do not have the luxury of being casual and disrespectful with our words and actions. When conflict associated with high school sports is the topic, educators must be focused on being the educators.

High school students are expected to act and speak like adolescents, and their parents are unfortunately often forgiven for behaving like teenagers. Educators, however, absolutely must be the adult in every conversation.

In many ways, the final rule of engagement guideline is the most important. School officials must not reinforce the misguided belief that they are in a position to honor all requests or solve everyone's problems—especially those related to high school sports. Some conflicts stemming from high school sports participation cannot be resolved, and in many cases these issues are not worthy of an educator's concern.

Consider an example involving a few high school boys hockey players and their parents. During warm-ups before games, as is the case for many high school sports teams, the boys hockey team was accustomed to having music (loud and aggressive tunes intended to get the blood pumping) played over the arena's sound system. Because Frank Sinatra and The Beach Boys fail to make the grade for our current batch of adolescents, adults (coaches and administrators) are generally not in a position to set the playlist for these warm-up tunes.

Coaches and administrators, however, are in a position to edit the playlist. When it became apparent that a few of the songs on the student-made cd contained words unfit for family consumption, despite the fact that the boys were warned to keep things classy, these school district employees refused to allow the cd to play. The result of such decision making was, unfortunately, predictable.

Several parents contacted the activities director to address their concerns about the music within the arena, not to thank school personnel for removing vulgarity from the premises, but rather to question why their boys had been stripped of a right to listen to motivating music before a hockey game.

One parent even hinted that the hockey team possibly lost a game because their adrenaline was not properly aligned due to the absence of a few Guns-N-Roses songs. The parents who contacted the activities director about the situation demanded a meeting to resolve the issue.

In an act of brilliance, the activities director refused to meet about the concern. Further, he reminded these parents that their sons were fortunate to be playing high school hockey and that removing the inappropriate cd from the arena's sound system was the smallest measure possible for the embarrassment of having a building full of mothers, fathers, grandparents, and children hear the f-bomb during a school-sanctioned event.

Sometimes we in education are obligated to be correct and remain strong, even if that means offending some of the crazies. Not every concern is worth our time; moreover, not every perceived problem is actually a problem. The solution for the boys hockey team and the warm-up music? To begin, most involved with the situation did not feel the players were maliciously intending to sneak vulgarity into the airwaves.

The solution, in this case, was to remove the cd, have a good chat with the young men who created it, and have them provide another capable of "pumping them up" without offending Grandma and Grandpa.

Nowhere in the answer to this ordeal involved a meeting with anyone's offended parents. My father, the same man coaches once sought for advice years ago, was fond of saying, "stupid people should feel uncomfortable when they talk."

This is not politically correct, it is not a way to win many friends, and it would be unwise for any school officials to use these words publicly. Yet, truth can be found in these words. Guidelines for high school sport participation are needed, if for no other reason, so that "smart" and "wise" have a fighting chance against the crazies.

THINGS TO REMEMBER

Why do our school districts offer sports to our students? There are countless benefits to high school sports participation, yet many adults, educators included, have forgotten the priceless connections tying the passion for sport to the necessity of school. Without the educational anchor (academics, discipline, guidelines, etc...), high school sports head toward the ridiculous and the regretful.

We want our student athletes to work diligently at sports, and we share with them the need to experience successes after such efforts have been given. This is fantastic, and high school sports in our country should continue to provide such opportunities. However, too many of us have failed to progress beyond pushing our student athletes to work hard and trying to win.

Many of us in education forget that our students are "playing" sports; we emphasize and prioritize the athletic efforts and accomplishments of these kids without realizing how incredibly shallow our concerns are for these student athletes.

To begin, losing a game is not the end of the world. Adolescent student athletes and some of their family members can lay awake at night about losing football, volleyball, soccer, basketball, and hockey games; those of us in education have bigger issues needing our attention.

Screaming and yelling and kicking and pouting because a collection of sixteen and seventeen year-old kids lost a game against a bunch of other sixteen and seventeen year-old kids? Our job is to make sure these young people overcome this approach to passion. We need to get serious about this.

Do we in education scream and yell, kick and pout, when one of our classroom lesson plans fails to deliver? Does our current AYP status have us up at 2:00 AM studying our school's charts and test scores so that we will perform better on the next round of tests? Of course not, so why in the world are many of us in education allowing a high school sport to dictate how we feel during our already limited family time at 10:00 PM on a Friday night?

Educators are best served applying some of the great common sense used in the classroom of our best teachers to handle high school sports: Work hard, play hard, prepare as best you can, and the results will be nothing more than a symptom of the processes taken to do things right. This system worked for John Wooden; it will work for coaching adolescents as well.

And as far as losing sleep about high school sports? Caring about one's job is admirable, certainly, but those of us working with student athletes need to ask ourselves if what we are caring about matches what we can control.

At their core, high school sports are symbols. Yes, sports matter, especially to the kids playing them, yet these sports almost always end up being a representation for all the things that truly matter in life. We condition our athletes to perform better on the field and court, of course, but deep down we also know we are preparing them for more than just a rivalry game against North High.

High school sports, like much of our curricular endeavors, are more about the bigger picture than the little details with which we become enamored. Just as it can be said that chemistry class was not a waste of time because most of us cannot remember Avogadro's number, so too we should conclude that a fantastic week of basketball practice is not a waste of time when the week is concluded with a gut wrenching loss. There is value in the process of working to get better at something.

Our practices and games are bits of essential foreshadowing for adolescents. We cannot teach a seventeen year-old how to work hard on his marriage, but we can teach him what it means to sacrifice some of his personal desires for the good of a team. Further, we can teach young people the importance of following through with a commitment.

Why else would we suspend high school student athletes from competition for mistakes like breaking a curfew or drinking alcohol? Kids who are caught smoking and drinking at a party are not suspended from math class, but we remove them from the game on Friday night. We do this because these kids know the rules and expectations beforehand, and educators cannot allow their student athletes to learn that promises made to teammates are irrelevant.

The whole high school sports process, in fact, is about more than the moment at hand. The crazies within our communities do not view things with this lens; these people live sports in the right here, right now. They want to know why their sons and daughters were made to feel the discomfort of a thirty point loss, and they want answers that night. They want immediate solutions to problems that required sixteen years to create—like lack of talent.

The crazies are infatuated with being entertained by the athletic successes of their children, and their shortsighted philosophies hold that their children can only benefit from high school sports if they play a leading role in a script that includes winning.

These people approach high school sports the same manner they watch ESPN, only they actually know the people for whom they are rooting. The crazies are the biggest challenge to high school sport success because they are fully stocked with two troublesome qualities:

1. They are adults and subsequently have had the capability to complain and be heard.
2. They are no more mature, at least regarding high school sports, than the children for whom they care.

It is for these reasons that high school sports must remain in the hands of great educators who insist that the connections between the classrooms and the locker rooms remain significant and influential. The following warning must be taken seriously: If or when high school sports move outside of the watchful eye of educators, we will never get them back.

Supplemental Pages: Suggestions for Parents

It is a fair assumption that both the educators within an independent school district and members of the community (especially parents) are serious about creating and maintaining healthy academic and extracurricular environments for children. Everyone involved with extracurricular activities should be striving for healthy relationships and communication practices between and among school officials, students, and families.

Further, it is vital that we adults participate in these activities with a healthy, harmonious passion, realizing that we must approach high school sports with rationality, modesty, and integrity. With these ideals in mind, the following are suggestions for all parents of high school student athletes.

PASSION

It is not appropriate for parents to have passion for high school sports equal to their son's or daughter's passion. High school sports belong to the students, and these young people should, as much as possible, own the experiences and emotions associated with these activities.

Our calling as parents is to keep our children level-headed, to guide them with a mature perspective during their adolescent years. Our children may, at times, want us to make their passions ours, but this is not what they need from us. After all, there is absolutely no need to fuel the already raging fire towards sports within our adolescent children.

PERSPECTIVE

Our children need to know that we care much more about them than we do about the sports they play. This sounds obvious, but it is essential to consider the way adolescents think regarding this issue. Sometimes, for example, caring the "right" way means caring in a way the child does not understand in that moment.

Again, these young people are passionate about their chosen sports—and that is fantastic. Our job is to support this passion, of course, but to also temper it by keeping losses, playing time, and other temporary failures in perspective by caring more about faith, family, academics, friendships, and character than whatever happens on the scoreboard.

Sports, furthermore, will serve our children well during these years. They will experience successes and failures, and both will be good for them in the long run. Our job is to keep things steady during the extremes our children experience—not take part in rocking the boat.

HOBBIES

Parents of high school student athletes should have their own hobbies, interests, and schedules outside of the high school sports dynamic. This perspective is a great model of healthy diversity for our children. High school sports belong to our kids, not us. We, therefore, are not wise to strive for equal ownership.

There is no need for a parent to attend a high school practice—this time belongs to the student athlete. With this, it is not only acceptable, but healthy, to miss a few games or more every season. Why? Ownership.

Adolescents do not need to be followed around the countryside and adored for their athletic accomplishments. Rather, they need the opportunity to figure out the balancing act between successes and conflict resolution on their own—and high school sports provide a wonderfully safe venue for this.

OLD-SCHOOL PARENTS

We owe it to our children and ourselves to remain the parents. We are not the coach, the choir director, or the cheerleading advisor—we are the parents. Our children are adolescents, so by definition they struggle with what they "want" us to be on a daily basis.

What we "need" to be, however, is irrelevant to our kids' wants. We need to be strong and consistent. Participation in high school sports will result in disappointments and failures for our children. It is not our job to fix these setbacks, or even to allow ourselves to feel stress about them. Our job is to be parents.

What does this mean? It means our children need to understand how fortunate they are to even have the opportunities they have in life. They, after all, live in a country that allows adolescent boys and girls to play sports for fun. In Israel, many of our kids would be too busy serving in the military to have a bad day playing soccer. There are students in our schools, as well, that can only dream of receiving the attention some of our student athletes glean on a daily basis.

They need to know that for all the talk about their great work ethic and winning attitude, they are equally indebted to the fact that they were born capable of running and jumping. Our job is to make certain they are more thankful than proud.

It also means that our kids need to know that we love them, but we are too damn busy to work 50 hours a week, travel 500 miles to watch a football game, and meet with the coaching staff and activities director about the fact that the coaches asked for the cell phones to be turned off during the bus ride. Our job is to point out that we now like the coach even more than we did the day before we heard that story.

Old-school parents do not lose sleep about losing to North High on Friday night; they may even have a laugh about the beat-down because they know better than to believe it was something more significant than a high school football game.

Old-school parents also do not worry about the opinions of their children as things relate to parenting. These parents can be friends with their kids when their kids are thirty, but for now they are willing to do or say the right things—regardless of its popularity among adolescents.

About the Author

John E. Tufte is professor of education at the University of Mary in Bismarck, North Dakota. He has taught and coached at the high school level, worked as a secondary administrator, and now presents to teachers, administrators, and parents about issues facing schools today.

Edwards Brothers Malloy
Thorofare, NJ USA
December 14, 2012